THE
STANDARD ENCYCLOPEDIA
OF
CARNIVAL GLASS
BY
BILL EDWARDS

The current values in this book should be used only as a guide. They are not intended to set prices, which vary from one section of the country to another. Auction prices as well as dealer prices vary greatly and are affected by condition as well as demand. Neither the Author nor the Publisher assumes responsibility for any losses that might be incurred as a result of consulting this guide.

Additional copies of this book may be ordered from:

COLLECTOR BOOKS
P.O. Box 3009
Paducah, Kentucky 42001

@ $24.95 Add $1.00 for postage and handling

Copyright: Bill Edwards, 1982
ISBN: 0-89145-187-0

This book or any part thereof may not be reproduced without the written consent of the Author and Publisher.

DEDICATION AND ACKNOWLEDGEMENTS

There simply isn't enough space to thank all the people who have helped by sharing their glass for my five previous books, but I would like to give a very special note of thanks to Mr. Don Moore, who has never failed to give full measure of aid whenever I asked. Much of the glass shown here is from his spectacular collection and I am deeply in his debt. To him I dedicate this book.

Also I'd like to express my gratitude to Singleton Bailey, Muriel and Bill Triplett, Ray Notley, Angela Hallam, Harold Ludeman, Don Doyle, Jack Wilson, Bill Carroll, Ed Garner, Joan Freeze, Norma Morrison, Dave Ackerman, Lee Briix, Grace and Byron Rinehart, Karma Vullo, Don Bauman, Bernice Fitzgerald, Mrs. Norman Guest, Bob Strasburger, Cecil and Floyd Whitley, Jim and LaNell Says, and Ted Parent, all who helped with this book.

And of course, a special thanks to my typist, Karen Hall.

AUTHOR'S NOTE

For the past ten years I have spent a major portion of my life learning about, living with, and writing about Carnival glass. Let me say that aside from the pure pleasure of handling so much of this beautiful glass, I've met so many very wonderful people, I feel my life has been enriched beyond measure by the experience.

I hope my many errors will be excused and my efforts to aid in the Carnival glass hobby by whatever talents the Lord has given me, remembered. This book is the culmination of all I've learned and a good deal of my soul is here.

I only hope it is adequate.

INTRODUCTION

For the benefit of the novice, Carnival glass is that pressed and iridized glass manufactured between 1905 and 1930. It was made by various companies in the United States, England, France, Germany, and Australia.

The iridization, unlike the costly art glass produced by Tiffany and his competitors, was achieved by a spray process on the surface of the glass before firing, thus producing a very beautiful product at a greatly reduced cost, giving the housewife a quality product well within her budget.

In addition, Carnival glass was the **last** hand-shaped glass mass-produced in America and remains as a beautiful reminder of the glassmaker's skills.

In this volume we will show the variety of shapes and colors of Carnival glass and will also attempt to define the patterns by manufacturer and for the first time, put the entire field of Carnival glass into one reference book for the collector.

It is my hope that this effort will bring new interest to this truly beautiful glass and stimulate its growth as a collectable; and my only regret is a lack of space to show every known pattern.

THE DUGAN STORY

In July, 1977, I was permitted to sort through the shards of the 1975 Helman diggings at the old Dugan dump site in Indiana, Pennsylvania. These shards were made available to me by William Heacock, noted author of Victorian Pattern glass books. The gesture was not only unique in the field of glass research, but generous beyond belief, for it afforded us the opportunity to "pool" our knowledge, compare notes and lend credence to the evidence offered by the shards.

This evidence, that Dugan did manufacture carnival glass for some time on its own, is indisputable; and that in close conjunction with Northwood Company in Wheeling, produced (on a sub-contract basis) carnival glass for the Northwood concern, is also evident.

I personally examined some 40-50 shards and have identified the following patterns from the Dugan dump site:

S-Repeat	Vineyard
Nautilis	Quill
Jeweled Heart	Leaf and Beads
Maple Leaf	Windflower
Coin Spot	Apple Blossom Twigs
Pastel Swan	Garden Path
Wreath of Roses Rosebowl	Rib and Panel Vase
Apple Blossoms	Fan
Vintage Grape	Diamond and Daisy Vase
Wreathed Cherry	Woodpecker Vase
Twig Vase (Beauty Bud Vase)	Stork and Rushes
Big Basketweave	Fluted Scrolls
Rambler Rose	Grape (and Cable)
Corinth	Peacock at the Fountain
Heavy Iris	Fanciful
Holly and Berry (handled sauce)	

As the reader can readily see, at least 26 of the above patterns are not trade-marked and could be Dugan patterns. Both Wreathed Cherry and Fan are patterns found with the Diamond trade-mark and are definitely Dugan items.

One other point of interest is that in addition to Fanciful and Apple Blossom Twigs, it appears the Roundup pattern most people credit to the Fenton Company is also a Dugan product since it has the same basketweave exterior as the other two patterns.

Of course the reader will have to decide for himself, the extent of Dugan's carnival glass production, but I'm convinced it was far greater than previously believed and only future research will clarify this exciting question.

I will be eternally grateful to Bill Heacock for sharing this information and personally consider it one of the major breakthroughs in carnival glass research in the last ten years.

In addition to the 1977 Dugan shards, a new group has recently been catalogued and even more patterns must be added to the list of products from this long-neglected company:

Lined Lattice Vase	Raindrops
Jewelled Heart	Double Stemmed Rose
Dahlia	Puzzle
Dogwood Sprays	Question Marks
Formal	Leaf Rays
Butterfly and Tulip	Vintage Banded
Malaga	Golden Grapes
Cherry (formerly Northwood Cherry)	Fisherman's Mug
Persian Garden	Heron Mug
Pony	Grape Delight
Beauty Bud Vase	Strawberry epergne
Many Fruits	Fish-net epergne
Lattice and Points	Farmyard
Constellation (Seaform)	

Attributions of these patterns are based on (1) shards identified, (2) ads in trade journals, (3) reverse patterns, (4) glass reproduced from molds purchased from the Dugan (Diamond) factory in the 1930's.

It is apparent the Dugan Company was one of the larger producers of Carnival glass (I'd guess more than 80 patterns) and certainly we must give it the recognition it deserves. Skeptics may challenge these findings, but I'm firmly convinced time will bear them out.

THE FENTON STORY

First organized in April 1905, the Fenton Art Glass Company didn't really materialize until the following July. At that time the glass decorating shop was opened in Martins Ferry, Ohio, in an abandoned factory rented by Frank L. Fenton and his brother, John (who was later to found the famous Millersburg Glass Company).

The next few months were occupied in obtaining financial backers, glass workers, buying land to be plotted into lots as a money-raising venture, and construction of their own plant in Williamstown, West Virginia. At times, everything seemed to go wrong and it wasn't until 1907 that the Company was "on its way."

From the first, the design abilities of Frank Fenton were obvious and each pattern seemed to bear his own special flair. He (along with Jacob Rosenthal who had come to the Fenton factory after fire had destroyed the renowned Indiana Tumbler and Goblet Company in Greentown, Indiana) was greatly responsible for sensing what the vast public admired in glass ornamentation.

In 1908 friction arose between the two brothers and John exited to pursue his dreams in Millersburg, Ohio. By this time, the Fenton process of iridization had taken the mass-scale art glass field by storm and "carnival glass" was on its way.

For the next fifteen years, the Fenton Company would produce the largest number of patterns ever in this beautiful product and huge amounts of iridized glass would be sent to the four corners of the world to brighten homes. While the Company made other decorative wears in custard, chocolate glass, mosaic inlaid glass, opalescent glass and stretch glass, nothing surpassed the quality and quantity of their iridized glass. Almost 150 patterns are credited to the Company in carnival glass alone and many more probably credited to others may be of Fenton origin.

All this is truly a remarkable feat and certainly Frank L. Fenton's genius must stand along side Harry Northwood's as inspiring.

THE IMPERIAL STORY

While the Imperial Glass Company of Bellaire, Ohio, was first organized in 1901 by a group of area investors, it wasn't until January 13, 1904, that the first glass was made; and not until nearly five years later the beautiful iridized glass we've come to call Carnival Glass was produced.

In the years between these dates, the mass market was sought, with a steady production of pressed glass water sets, single tumblers, jelly jars, lamp shades and chimneys, and a full assortment of table items such as salt dips, pickle trays, condiment bottles and oil cruets.

All of this was a prelude of course, to the art glass field which swept the country and in 1909 Imperial introduced their iridescent line of blown lead lustre articles as well as the Nuruby, Sapphire and Peacock colors of Carnival Glass.

As was quite evident then, as now, this proved to be the hallmark of their production. Huge quantities of the iridized glass were designed, manufactured and sold to the mass market-place across America and the European Continent for the next decade in strong competition with the other art glass factories. Especially sought was the market in England, early in 1911.

In quality, Imperial must be ranked second only to the fine glass produced by the Millersburg Company and certainly, in design, is on an equal with the great Northwood Company. Only the Fenton Company produced more recognized patterns and has outlasted them in longevity (the Imperial Glass Company became a subsidiary of the Lenox Company in 1973).

Along the way came the fabulous art glass line called "Imperial Jewels" in 1916. This was an iridescent product often in free hand worked with a "stretch" effect. This is so popular today, many glass collectors have large collections of this alone.

In 1929, Imperial entered the machine glass era and produced its share of what has come to be called Depression Glass and, in the early 1960's, the Company revived their old molds and reproduced many of the old iridized patterns as well as creating a few new ones for the market that was once again invaded by "Carnival Glass Fever." While many collectors purchased these items, purists in Carnival Glass collecting have remained loyal to the original and without question, the early years of Carnival Glass production at the Imperial Company will always be their golden years.

One interesting footnote to the Imperial Story is that apparently one of the mold designers left the Company at the end World War I and returned to his native England. We know this because several patterns known to have been made at Imperial from 1910-1916 were later produced in England. These patterns are Scroll Embossed, Curved Star (called Cathedral on English items) and Headdress. The Diving Dolphins compote with Scroll Embossed interior, long felt to be Imperial is actually of English origin! To add to the confusion, I've recently learned the Cosmos and Cane pattern is found with a Headdress interior!

THE MILLERSBURG STORY

On May 20, 1909 John Fenton poured his first glass, officially opening the Millersburg Glass Company, and for the next twenty-four months produced the beautiful glass we now call "Millersburg." The opening ended a thirteen month search for an appropriate factory site, construction of a modern factory, sale of stocks and employment of skilled glass workers and designers.

Mr. Fenton, at the age of 38 (along with his brother Robert), had decided to leave the Fenton Art Glass Company and strike out on his own. Always a glib talker, a talented promoter and a "cracker-jack" salesman, he liked to "run the show" and felt the need to test himself.

After much deliberation, a 54 acre site was secured by option, home lots were platted and sold to gain capital and the ground for the factory was broken on September 14, 1908. Besides the main building which housed a 14 pot furnace, there was a smaller building used for packing and shipping of the finished product. Upon incorporation, John Fenton became president, with H. W. Stanley as vice-president and treasurer, Robert Fenton as secretary and H. F. Weber as general sales manager (Robert Fenton left in 1910 to eventually rejoin the family glass company in Williamstown, West Virginia).

For the first few months, the Millersburg company produced crystal and glass iridized with the Fenton process. Then on January 4, 1910, after seven months of experimentation, the fantastic process of iridization that would be known as "radium" finish was introduced. (Many insiders credit Millersburg worker, Oliver Phillips along with his sons, Dean, Dale and Jesse of Finley, Ohio for the discovery of the radium process. Mr. Phillips had helped begin the Cambridge Glass company earlier and was greatly responsible for the close working relationship between the Millersburg and Cambridge factories.)

Later that month, at a glass exposition at the Fort Pitt Hotel in Pittsburg, a Millersburg display of radium finish glass was judged the finest entry of the exposition and greatly excited the entire glass industry. From then until its demise, the Millersburg factory concentrated its efforts on this product, making bowls, table sets, vases, water sets, and novelty items in rich hues of green, marigold, amethyst, vaseline, purple and blue (throughout our research, we have authenticated *no* examples of red, ice blue, ice green, aqua opalescent, smokey, pink, or white from the Millersburg factory).

Although they had their own mold makers, with the success brought by the new glass process, it was decided operations would be expanded. The Hipkins Novelty Mold Company of Martins Ferry, Ohio was contracted and immediately added new molds to the Millersburg line, producing them for an 18 month period on a credit basis. During this period, large amounts of Millersburg glass were sold, mostly through the New York wholesale house, Butler Brothers, and one order of $80,000.00 is known to have been taken. Glass was shipped to England, the continent, and even Australia.

In June of 1910, the world famous "Millersburg Court House" souvenir bowl was produced as a gesture of thanks for those who had assisted earlier in laying the gas lines to the factory (still later would come other items of appreciation to Holmes County citizens such as the Peoples Vase).

In a few months, it became painfully obvious the company, although a success in glass production, was in grave financial trouble. John Fenton, while a personable, respected glass technician, was not a business manager. His fondness for extravagant living, his habit of gifts to all factory visitors and his showering of items of glass on the town and surrounding areas were much to blame. This, coupled with the eighteen months of mold bills owed to the Hipkins Company and the keen competition in the industry were just too much. After a lawsuit was filed by Hipkins, the Millersburg Glass Company declared bankruptcy in June, 1911 and was consequently sold to Samuel B. Fair for $14,000.00 on September 23 of that year.

Mr. Fair formed the Radium Glass Company in October, 1911, retained Mr. Fenton as vice-president and production advisor and operated for six months, making radium finish carnival glass only. Though his efforts were valiant, he could not regain the momentum the company had once enjoyed. Many of the glass workers had moved to other companies, financial backing was not to be had and the company's reputation had suffered greatly. In May of that year, the doors were closed and the last piece of Millersburg glass had been produced.

In succeeding years, the area's citizens, many who had lost life-time savings in the venture, were understandably bitter; few felt John Fenton had used their investments wisely. In all fairness, one must admit his ability to spend money was extraordinary and perhaps the company could have survived if he had been more prudent financially. However the competition in glass production was tremendously stiff and the "big three" controlled much of the market from the beginning.

Most of the Millersburg glass was stored in attics and basements to be forgotten or simply thrown away. Only in the last decade has the true worth of Millersburg glass been realized and fortunate are those who wisely saved their pieces. We've come full cycle and once again Millersburg is the queen of Carnival Glass.

THE NORTHWOOD STORY

An entire book could be written about Harry Northwood, using every superlative the mind could summon and still fail to do justice to the man; a genius in his field. Of course Harry had an advantage in the glass industry since his father, John Northwood, was a renowned English glass maker.

Harry Northwood came to America in 1880 and first worked for Hobbs, Brockunier and Company of Wheeling, West Virginia, an old and established glass producing firm. For five years Harry remained in Wheeling, learning his craft and dreaming his dreams.

In 1886, he left Hobbs, Brockunier and was employed by the LaBelle Glass Company of Bridgeport, Ohio, where he advanced to the position of Manager in 1887. A few months later a devastating fire destroyed much of the LaBelle factory and it was sold in 1888.

Harry next went to work for the Buckeye Glass Company of Martin's Ferry, Ohio. Here he remained until 1896 when he formed the Northwood Company at Indiana, Pennsylvania. Much of the genius was now being evidenced and such products as the famous Northwood custard glass date from this period.

In 1899 Northwood entered the National Glass combine only to become unhappy with its financial problems and in 1901 he broke away to become an independent manufacturer once again. A year later, he bought the long-idle Hobbs, Brockunier plant and for the next couple of years there were two Northwood plants.

Finally, in 1904, Northwood leased the Indiana, Pennsylvania plant to its managers, Thomas E. Dugan and W. G. Minnemeyer, who changed the name of the plant to the Dugan Glass Company (in 1913 the plant officially became known as the Diamond Glass Company and existed as such until it burned to the ground in 1931).

In 1908, Harry Northwood, following the success of his student, Frank L. Fenton, in the iridized glass field, marketed his first Northwood iridescent glass and Northwood carnival glass was born. For a ten year period, carnival glass was the great American "craze" and even at the time of Harry Northwood's death in 1921, small quantities were still being manufactured. It had proved to be Northwood's most popular glass, the jewel in the crown of a genius, much of it marked with the well-known trade-mark.

MINOR AMERICAN COMPANIES

Besides the five major producers of Carnival glass in America, several additional companies produced small amounts of iridized glass.

These companies include: the Cambridge Glass Company of Cambridge, Ohio; the Jenkins Glass Company of Kokomo, Indiana; the Westmoreland Glass Company of Grapeville, Pennsylvania; the Fostoria Glass Company of Moundsville, West Virginia; the Heisey Glass Company of Newark, Ohio; the McKee-Jeanette Glass Company of Jeanette, Pennsylvania; and the U.S. Glass Company of Pittsburgh, Pennsylvania.

The Cambridge Company was the "leader" of the lesser companies and the quality of their iridized glass was of a standard equal to that of the Millersburg Glass Company. Actually, there appears to have been a close working relationship between the two concerns and some evidence exists to lead us to believe some Cambridge patterns were iridized at the Millersburg factory. The Venetian vase is such an item. Known Cambridge patterns are:

Horn of Plenty	Inverted Thistle
Sweetheart	Double Star (Buzz Saw)
Buzz Saw cruet	Near Cut Souvenir
Cologne Bottle	Proud Puss
Forks Cracker Jar	Tomahawk
Inverted Feather	Toy Punch Set
Inverted Strawberry	Venetian

Near-Cut Decanter

Many of the Cambridge patterns are beautiful near-cut designs or patterns intaglio; and while amethyst and blue are colors rarely found, most Cambridge Carnival glass was made in green and marigold.

The Jenkins Glass Company made only a handful of Carnival glass patterns, mostly in marigold color and nearly all patterns in intaglio with a combination of flower and near-cut design. Their known patterns are:

Cane and Daisy Cut	Fleur De Lis Vase
Cut Flowers	Oval Star and Fan
Diamond and Daisy Cut	Stippled Strawberry

The Westmoreland Company also made quality Carnival glass in limited amounts. Known patterns are:

Checkerboard	Strutting Peacock
Footed Drape	Pillow and Sunburst
Footed Shell	Shell and Jewel
Basketweave and Cable	

The Fostoria Company had two types of iridized glass. The first was their Taffeta Lustre line which included console sets, bowls and candlesticks; the second was their brocaded patterns which consisted of an acid cutback design, iridized and decorated with gold. These patterns include:

Brocaded Acorns	Brocaded Palms
Brocaded Daffodils	Brocaded Roses

Brocaded Summer Garden

Heisey made very few iridized items and those found have a light, airy luster. Patterns known are:

Covered Frog	Heisey #357
Covered Turtle	Heisey Flute
Heisey Tray Set	Panelled Heisey

The McKee-Jeanette Company had a few Carnival glass patterns as follows:

Aztec	Rock Crystal
Heart Band Souvenir	Sea Gulls Bowl
Lutz	Snow Fancy

Hobnail Panels

The U.S. Glass Company was a combine of seventeen companies, headquartered in Pittsburgh, Pennsylvania. Their plants were usually designated by letters and it is nearly impossible to say what item came from which factory, however some of the patterns we have classified as U.S. Glass are:

Beads and Bars	Louisville Shrine Champagne
Daisy in Oval Panels	Rochester Shrine Champagne
Field Thistle	Shrine toothpick
Golden Harvest	Palm Beach
New Orleans Shrine Champagne	Vintage Wine
Feather Swirl	Butterfly Tumbler

In addition to all the glass produced by these minor concerns, specialty glass houses contributed their share of iridized glass in the large Gone-With-the-Wind lamps, shades, chimneys, etc.; as well as minute amounts of iridized glass from Libby, Anchor-Hocking, Tiffin, Devilbiss, Hig-Bee, and Jeanette are known.

It is not possible in our limited space to show all these patterns from the smaller makers, but we'll try to give a sampling from many of them.

In addition, many patterns in Carnival glass have not been attributed to definite producers at this time and so you will find a few items shown where we must say "maker unknown." While we wish this didn't have to be, sooner or later, these too will find their proper place in the history of Carnival glass.

ENGLISH CARNIVAL GLASS

When iridized glass caught the buyer's fancy in this country, the major companies (especially Imperial and Fenton) began to ship Carnival glass to England, Europe, and Australia and it wasn't long until the glass houses there began to enter the iridized field. In England, the chief producer of this glass was the Sowerly Company of Gateshead-on-Tyne. However other concerns made some iridized glass including Gueggenheim, Ltd., of London and Davisons of Gateshead.

The movement of Carnival glass in England began later than in America and lasted about five years after sales had diminished in this country. Many shapes were made including bowls, vases, compotes, and table pieces. However water sets and punch sets were pretty much overlooked and only a few examples of these have come to light. Colors in English glass were mainly confined to marigold, blue, and amethyst, but an occasional item in green does appear. The pastels apparently were not popular for few examples exist.

Here then is a list of known English patterns and its volume may surprise many collectors:

African Shield
Apple Panels
Art Deco
Banded Grape and Leaf
Beaded Hearts
Buddha
Cane and Scroll
Cathedral (Curved Star)
Cathedral Arches (Hobstar and Cathedral)
Chariot
Classic Arts (Egyptian)
Cosmos and Cane
Covered Hen
Covered Swan
Daisy Block
Daisy and Cane
Diamond Ovals
Diving Dolphins
Fans
Feathered Arrow
File
Fine Cut Rings
Fish vase (possibly French)
Flower Block
Flute sherbet
Footed Prism Panels
Grape and Cherry
Hand vase
Heavy Prisms
Hobstar Cut Triangles

Hobstar Reversed
Illinois Daisy
Inca vase
Intaglio Daisy
Kokomo
Lattice Heart
Lea (and varients)
May Basket
Moonprint
My Lady's Powderbox
Pebble and Fan
Pineapple
Pinwheel
Pinwheel vase
Rose Garden
Sacic ashtray
Saint candlestick
Sea Gull vase
Signet
Spiralex
Split Diamond
Star coaster
Stippled Diamond Swag
Sunflower and Diamond
Sunken Daisy
Thistle and Thorn
Tiny Berry tumbler
Triads
Vining Leaf
Western Thistle

AUSTRALIAN CARNIVAL GLASS

Just as England caught the "fever," so did the populace of Australia and in 1918, the Crystal Glass Works, Ltd., of Sydney began to produce a beautiful line of iridized glass, whose finish ranks with the very best; mostly in bowls and compotes, but with occasional table items and two water sets known.

Australian Carnival glass is confined to purple, marigold, and an unusual amber over aqua finish and patterns known are:

Australian Swan
Banded Diamonds
Butterflies and Bells
Butterflies and Waratah
Butterfly Bower
Butterfly Bush
Flannel Flower
Flannel Berry
Kangaroo (and variants)
Kingfisher
Magpie
Crystal Cut
Australian Grape
Beaded Spears

Kiwi
Kookaburra (and variants)
Pin-Ups
Emu (Ostrich)
Rose Panels
S-Band
Sun Gold Epergne
Thunderbird (Shrike)
Waterlily and Dragonfly
Wild Fern
Golden Cupid
Feathered Flowers

ACANTHUS

Found both in many shaped bowls and plates, the Acanthus was once considered to be a Millersburg pattern, but old Imperial catalogs have proved its origin as Imperial. The colors are usually marigold or smoke, but I show the pattern in green and I'm sure amethyst is a strong possibility. The mold work is good, the glass quality and the iridescence very good.

ACORN

It would be hard to imagine a more naturalistic pattern than this. Realistic acorns and oak leaves arranged in three groupings, filling much of the allowed space, form a very pleasing design. Acorn is found on both bowls and plates in a wide range of colors including marigold, amethyst, green, red, vaseline, ice blue and iridized milk glass.

ACORN

Rarely found, this beautiful compote is typically Millersburg in several respects. First, the shape of the stem and the clover-leaf type base are found on several compotes of the Ohio company. Add to that the fine detail of the design, the excellent workmanship and if that isn't enough the typical Millersburg colors of green or amethyst and that should convince anyone. A rare vaseline is known, but a marigold Acorn compote would be a real find.

ACORN BURRS

Other than the famous Northwood Grape and their Peacock at Fountain pattern, Acorn Burrs is probably the most representative of the factory's work and one eagerly sought by Carnival Glass collectors. The pattern background is that of finely done oak bark while the leaves are those of the chestnut oak. The mold-work is well done and the coloring ranks with the best. Acorn Burrs is found in a wide range of colors and shapes and always brings top dollar.

ADVERTISING ITEMS

These come in dozens of varieties, several shapes and colors, and it would be impossible in our limited space to show them all. Advertising items were a much welcomed area of business by **all** carnival glass makers because they were a guaranteed source of income without the usual cost-lost factor of unsold stock. Also they could often be made with less care since they were to be given away; old molds could often be utilized, avoiding expensive new molds. Many Northwood advertising items were small plates, with simple floral designs.

AFRICAN SHIELD

While toothpick holders were not in style in England, at least this one fine example exists. The African Shield toothpick is very good glass with sparkling color. It is 2⅞" tall and 3¼" wide at the top.

Acanthus

Acorn

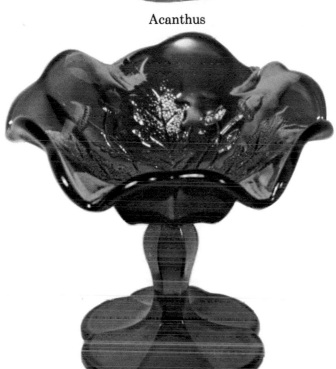

Acorn

Acorn Burrs

Advertising Items

African Shield

11

AGE HERALD

Once thought to be a Millersburg item, we now are convinced the Age Herald bowls and plates were made by Fenton. Found only in amethyst, the Age Herald was a give-away item from the Birmingham, Alabama newspaper. It has an exterior pattern of wide panels and is a scarce and expensive pattern.

AMARYLLIS

This unusual compote is a treasure for several reasons. First is the size (2¼″ tall, 5¼″ wide). The shape is roughly triangular, rising from a slightly domed base. The underside carries the Poppy Wreath pattern and the only colors reported are a deep purple, cobalt blue and marigold.

Amaryllis is a rather scarce Northwood pattern and isn't often mentioned in carnival glass discussions. It is, however, a unique and interesting addition to any collection.

APPLE AND PEAR INTAGLIO

Like its cousin, the Strawberry Intaglio, this rather rare bowl is a product of the Northwood Company and is seen mostly in crystal or goofus glass. The example shown measures 9¾″ in diameter and is 2¾″ tall. The glass is ½″ thick!

APPLE BLOSSOM TWIGS

This is a very popular pattern, especially in plates where the design is shown to full advantage. The detail is quite nice with fine mold work, much like that of Acorn Burrs. Found mostly in marigold, peach and purple, Apple Blossom Twigs has as its exterior pattern, the Big Basketweave pattern. Shards in this pattern at the Dugan site have been identified.

APPLE BLOSSOMS

Found only in small bowls or plates, Apple Blossoms seems to be an average carnival glass pattern, produced for a mass market in large quantities. Most often seen in Marigold, it is occasionally found in vivid colors as well as pastels, especially white. A quarter size chunk of this pattern in white was found at the Dugan dump site in 1975.

APPLE PANELS

There is some dispute about the origin of this cute breakfast set; some say Imperial, others England. I personally feel Apple Panels is a British Pattern, because so many examples come from there, however the pattern is known in green which is unusual for English glass.

The pattern is all intaglio and no other shapes are known. Green and marigold are the only reported colors.

Age Herald

Amaryllis

Apple and Pear Intaglio

Apple Blossom Twigs

Apple Blossoms

Apple Panels

APPLE TREE

It certainly is a pity Fenton chose to use this realistic pattern on water sets only. It would have made a beautiful table set or punch set. Apple Tree is available in marigold, cobalt blue and white and I've seen a rare vase whimsey formed from the pitcher with the handle omitted. The coloring is nearly always strong and bright.

APRIL SHOWERS

Like the bubbles in a carbonated soft drink, the tiny beads seem to float over this very interesting vase pattern. Found in all sizes from 5″ to 14″ April Showers is sometimes found with Peacock Tail pattern on the interior. The colors are marigold, blue, purple, green and white. The top edge is usually quite ruffled in the Fenton manner.

ARCS

This pattern is often confused by beginning collectors with the Scroll Embossed pattern and it's easy to see why. Perhaps they were designed by the same person since they are both Imperial patterns. Arcs is found on bowls of average size, often with an exterior of File pattern, and on compotes with a geometric exterior. The usual colors are marigold or a brilliant amethyst, but green does exist as does smoke.

ART DECO

We don't often see such a plain carnival pattern, but this one has a good deal of interest, despite its lack of design. The very modern look was all the rage in the art deco age so I've named this cute little bowl in that manner. I don't know who the English manufacturer was.

AUSTRALIAN FLOWER SET

Used like the Water Lily and Dragonfly flower set, this Australian beauty has no design except the slender thread border on the bowl's exterior. The iridescence is fantastic, as you can see.

AUSTRALIAN GRAPE

I can't confirm the existence of a pitcher to match this tumbler, but I'd guess there is. The marigold color is weak, but the mold work is nice. It is from Australia, where it is called Vineyard Harvest.

Apple Tree

April Showers

Arcs

Art Deco

Australian Flower Set

Australian Grape

15

BANDED GRAPE AND LEAF

Here is the **only** water set I've heard about in English glass, besides the Western Thistle. As you can see the design is quite good and the color better than average. The only color I've seen is marigold and at least two sets of this pattern are in American collections.

BASKET

Novelty items are a very important area of glass production and this little item is one of the best known. Standing on four sturdy feet, the Northwood Basket is about 5¾" tall and 5" across. Often the basket is simply round but sometimes one finds an example that has been pulled into a six-sided shape. Made in a wide range of colors, including marigold, purple, vaseline, cobalt, ice green, ice blue, aqua and white, this is a popular pattern.

BASKETWEAVE

This Dugan pattern is found on the exterior of Fanciful and Round-up bowls, the base pattern for the Persian Garden two-piece fruit bowls and for vases as shown, as well as a miniature handled basket. Colors are marigold, amethyst, blue, peach opalescent, and white.

BASKETWEAVE AND CABLE

Much like the Shell and Jewel breakfast set from the same company, the Westmoreland Basketweave and Cable is a seldom found pattern and surely must have been made in limited amounts. The mold work is excellent and the luster satisfactory. Colors are marigold (often pale), amethyst, green, and rarely white.

BEADED ACANTHUS

It's hard to believe this outstanding pattern was made in this one shape only, but to date I've heard of no other. This milk pitcher, like the Poinsettia, measures 7" tall and has a base diameter of 3¾". It is found mostly on marigold glass or smoke but a very outstanding green obviously exists and I suspect amethyst is also a possibility. The coloring is usually quite good and the iridescence is what one might expect from the Imperial Company.

BEADED BAND AND OCTAGON LAMP

Here is a seldom-seen oil lamp that is really very attractive. The coloring is adequate but watery, indicating 1920's production. It was reportedly made in two sizes, 7½" and 9¾", but I can't confirm this. The maker is unknown.

Banded Grape and Leaf

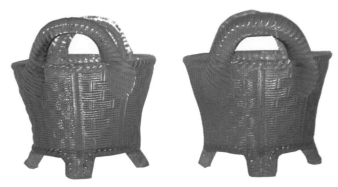

Basket

Basketweave

Basketweave and Cable

Beaded Acanthus

Beaded Band and
Octagon Lamp

BEADED BASKET

While the Beaded Basket is quite plentiful, especially in marigold, its origin has always been a little in doubt and I'm placing it here as a questionable Dugan pattern. Actually, the design qualities are quite good and the mold work superior, so any company could well be proud of these cuties. The colors are marigold, purple, blue and smoke, with the blue most difficult to find. Green may exist but I haven't heard of one, nor have I had any other pastels reported, except the rare vaseline shown.

BEADED BULLS EYE

There are several variations of this vase pattern, often caused by the "pulling" or "slinging" to obtain height. Nevertheless, the obvious rows of bull-eyes on the upper edge serve to establish identity. Found mostly in marigold, these Imperial vases are not easily found.

BEADED CABLE

The Beaded Cable rosebowl has long been a favorite with collectors for it is a simple yet strong design, made with all the famous Northwood quality. Usually about 4″ tall, these rosebowls stand on three sturdy legs. The prominent cable intertwines around the middle and is, of course, edged by beads. Nearly all pieces are marked and are made in a wide variety of colors. Of course, these pieces are sometimes opened out to become a candy dish, like many Northwood footed items.

BEADED PANELS COMPOTE

Here is one of the most imaginative compotes I've seen and while it is attributed to Davisons of Gateshead, the peach opalescent coloring leads me to believe this was a product of Dugan. If this is the case, most were shipped to England for that's where the majority are found.

BEADED SHELL

Known also in custard glass, Beaded Shell is one of the older Dugan patterns and is found in a variety of shapes, including berry sets, table sets, water sets and mugs. Colors are purple, blue, green, marigold and white with blue and purple somewhat more easily found. Beaded Shell is seldom marked.

BEADED SPEARS

This previously unlisted, Australian water set is a very scarce and beautiful pattern. Besides the peaks of stylized prisms, there are sections of fine file work with unusual circles of plain glass. Other colors and shapes aren't known to me, but certainly may exist.

Beaded Basket

Bullseye Beads

Beaded Cable

Beaded
Panels
Compote

Beaded Shell

Beaded Spears

21

BEADED SWIRL

Besides the attractive compote shown, this pattern has been seen in a covered sugar, covered butter dish, and a milk pitcher, all in a good, rich marigold. I've been told the maker was Davisons of Gateshead, but haven't confirmed this. At any rate, the design is a good one and the color very rich.

BEADS

It's really a shame this pattern isn't found more often and is restricted to the exterior of average size bowls, because it is a well-balanced, attractive item, especially on vivid colors. Combining three motifs — daisy-like flowers, petalish blooms and beads — this pattern, while not rare, is certainly not plentiful and is a desirable Northwood item.

BEAUTY BUD VASE (TWIGS)

The most distinctive feature of this vase is of course the twig-like feet, intended to be tree roots and these vases are found in sizes from 3½″ to 11″ tall.

Marigold is the most plentiful color and often only the top shows any hues at all, but the tiny purple version is a beauty and is much sought by vase collectors. Dugan Glass.

BELLAIRE SOUVENIRS

This curious bowl measures 7″ in diameter and is roughly 2½″ deep. The lettering and little bell are all interior work, while the fine ribbing is on the outside. Just when this bowl was given or why remains a mystery to me, but I'm quite sure it would have great appeal to the collector of lettered glass. This was made by Imperial.

BELLS AND BEADS

Shards of this pattern turned up in the Helman digs, so we know this is another Dugan pattern. Found in small bowls, plates, hat shapes, nappies, compotes, and a handled gravy boat, Bells and Beads' colors are marigold, blue, amethyst, green and peach opalescent.

BERNHEIMER BOWL

The only difference between this much sought bowl and the famous Millersburg Many Stars pattern is of course the advertising center, consisting of a small star and the words: Bernheimer Brothers. This replaces the usual large star and demonstrates how a clever mold designer can capitalize on a good design. While not nearly as plentiful as the Many Stars bowls, the Bernheimer bowls, oddly enough are found in blue.

Beaded Swirl

Beads

Beauty
Bud
Vase
(Twigs)

Bellaire Souvenirs

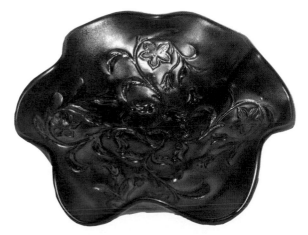

Bells and Beads

Bernheimer Bowl

BIG FISH

If there is a single bowl pattern on which the Millersburg reputation could rest, this wouldn't be a bad choice. Like the Millersburg Peacock, the mold work is outstanding, and the realistic portrayal of the species is exceptional. Each scale, each flower petal is so realistically done that the fish almost seems ready to leap from the glass. Here again, a wide variety of bowl shapes were produced and it is not unusual to see round, square or three cornered ones. Often, the amethyst is a little pale but the green is marvelous and my personal favorite. Again, we find a wide panel exterior with a rayed base.

BIG THISTLE PUNCH BOWL

I could spend pages raving about this very superb Millersburg rarity, but let me simply say I consider it the most beautiful of *all* the carnival glass punch bowls. Two are known and both are amethyst. One has a flared top while the other is straight up. Needless to say, the glass is clear, the mold work superior and the iridescence beyond belief.

BIRD WITH GRAPES

This unusual wall vase is somewhat similar to the woodpecker vase in concept and I'd guess it too is a product of the Dugan factory but can't be positive. The coloring is a pale marigold with an amber tint.

BIRDS AND CHERRIES

Found quite often on bon bons and compotes, this realistic Fenton pattern is usually found on rare berry sets and very rare 10″ plates. The birds, five in number, remind me of grackles or blackbirds. I've heard of this pattern in marigold, blue, green, amethyst, white, pastel-marigold and vaseline.

BLACKBERRY

Found often as an interior pattern on the open edge basketweave hat shape Fenton produced in great numbers, Blackberry is a very realistic pattern, gracefully molded around the walls of the hat. It is known in many colors including marigold, cobalt blue, green, amethyst, ice blue, ice green, vaseline and red. The example shown is blue with marigold open edge.

BLACKBERRY

This rare Fenton whimsey is shaped from the two-row open edge basket with Blackberry pattern interior. The vase has been shaped into a 8¼″ tall beauty. The only color reported is a beautiful cobalt blue but others may certainly exist.

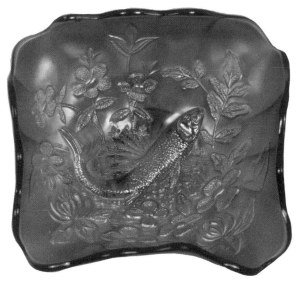

Big Fish

Big Thistle Punch Bowl

Bird With Grapes

Birds and Cherries

Blackberry

Blackberry Whimsey Vase

BLACKBERRY

While several companies had a try at a Blackberry pattern, Northwood's is one of the better ones and quite distinctive. The pattern covers most of the allowed space, be it the interior of a 6″ compote or an 8½″ footed bowl. Combined with the latter is often a pattern called Daisy and Plume. The colors are marigold, purple, green and white.

BLACKBERRY BANDED

Like many Fenton patterns, Blackberry Banded is limited to the hat shape, and without an exterior pattern. These ruffled hats are usually between 3¼″ and 3¾″ tall, with a base diameter of 2½″. Found mostly in marigold or cobalt blue, they are rarely found in green and, as you can see, there is a rare milk glass with marigold iridization.

BLACKBERRY BLOCK

Make no mistake about it — this is a much underrated water set! Just why it hasn't become more treasured by collectors puzzles me, because it is well made, pretty and quite scarce. Found in marigold, green and cobalt blue, I suspect white was made too, but haven't verified a set in this color yet. Manufactured by Fenton.

BLACKBERRY BRAMBLE

A very available pattern on bowls and compotes, Blackberry Bramble is a very close cousin to the Fenton Blackberry pattern, but has more leaves, berries and thorny branches. The bowls are rather small with diameters of 6″ to 8¼″ and the compotes are of average size. Colors are marigold, green and cobalt blue, but others may certainly exist.

BLACKBERRY SPRAY

I've always felt this a poorly designed pattern, but others may disagree. There isn't too much graceful about the four separate branches and the fruit isn't spectacular. Nevertheless, it can be found on hat shapes, bon-bons and compotes, in marigold, cobalt blue, green, amethyst, aqua and red. The aqua does not have opalescence, at least the examples I've seen.

BLACKBERRY WREATH

Apparently one of the early Millersburg patterns Blackberry Wreath is found more often than not without the radium finish. Oddly enough, the basic pattern is like the Millersburg Strawberry except for the center berry and leaf; however, the moldwork is not as distinct and the glass doesn't have the clarity of the Strawberry pattern. Nevertheless, Blackberry Wreath is a nicely proportioned pattern, especially on the larger bowls. The exterior is usually decorated with a wide panel design and has a many-rayed star on the base, exactly like the Millersburg Peacock and Urn variant.

Blackberry

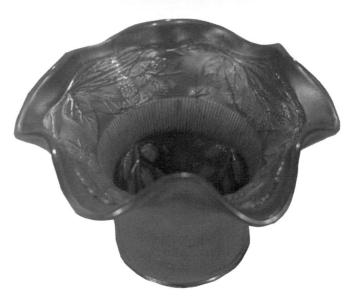

Blackberry Banded

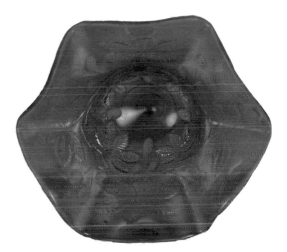

Blackberry Bramble

Blackberry
Black

Blackberry Spray

Blackberry Wreath

BLOSSOMS AND BAND

While Blossoms and Band is a very undistinguished pattern, its origin is questionable. Found primarily on berry sets in marigold, a car vase is also known, as shown. The design is quite simple, with a row of blossoms, stems and leaves above a band of thumbprints and prisms. The color has a good deal of pink in the marigold, much like English glass. The mold work is adequate but far from outstanding. Needless to say, this is not the same pattern as that found on the Millersburg Wild Rose lamps that are often called by the same name. This is possibly an Imperial pattern.

BLOSSOMTIME

Even if this outstanding compote were not marked, we'd surely assign it to the Northwood company because it is so typical of their work. The flowers, the thorny branches (twisted into a geometrical overlapping star) and the curling little branchlets are all nicely done and are stippled, except for the branchlets. The background is plain and contrasts nicely. Blossomtime is combined with an exterior pattern called Wild Flower and is found in marigold, purple, green and pastels. The stem is quite unusual, being twisted with a screw-like pattern. Blossomtime is a scarce pattern and always brings top dollar.

BLUEBERRY

May I say in the beginning, I'm quite prejudiced about this Fenton water set, for I think it is outstanding in both design and execution. What a shame it wasn't made in other shapes such as a table set. I've heard of Blueberry in marigold, cobalt blue and white only but that doesn't mean it wasn't made in other colors.

BO PEEP MUG AND PLATE

While the Bo Peep mug is simply scarce, the plate is a quite rare item, seldom sold or traded from one collection to another. The color is good marigold and reminds us of that found on most of the Fenton Kitten items. Of course, all children's items in glass were subjected to great loss through breakage, but I doubt if large amounts of the Bo Peep pattern were made to begin with; so of course small quantities have survived.

BOGGY BAYOU
(PANELLED DIAMOND AND BOWS)

This interesting Fenton pattern is called Panelled Diamond and Bows by Mrs. Presznick but William Heacock identifies it as Boggy Bayou so I listed both names here. As you can see, it has a roughly geometric panel of diamonds with propeller-like fillers between. These are listed in sizes from 7″ to 11″. The colors I've heard about are marigold, green, blue, amethyst, and white, but probably there are others.

BORDER PLANTS

Again, here is a pattern long regarded as a Fenton product, but it is actually from the Dugan factory. The colors I've seen are amethyst and peach opalescent, but others may exist. The bowl can be found either flat or footed.

Blossom Time

Blossoms and Band

Blueberry

Bo Peep Mug and Plate

Boggy Bayou (Panelled Diamond and Bows)

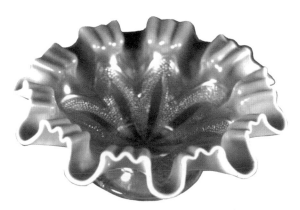

Border Plants

BOUQUET

If you look quite closely at this bulbous water set, you'll notice several common devices used by the Fenton Company, such as fillers of scales surrounding an embroidery ring. No other shapes exist and the water set is found in marigold, blue, and white. The mold work is quite good and the colors typically Fenton.

BOUTONNIERE

This little beauty had me going for quite a while because in design it looked so much like a Northwood product, but after examining more than a dozen of these compotes, I'm sure it is a Millersburg product. It usually has an extra fine radium finish and is most often seen in amethyst. And although I haven't seen one, I've been told there is a variation sometimes found with a different stem and base. Boutonniere is also found in marigold and green.

HEISEY BREAKFAST SET

While it isn't so marked, I'd guess this very attractive marigold breakfast set was a Heisey product. The coloring is very dark and rich and the handles are like those on known Heisey products.

BROCADED ACORNS

The lacy effects of all these brocaded patterns by the Fostoria company are a joy to behold. This was achieved by an acid-cutback process and after the iridescence was fired a gold edging was applied. Found in several shapes, Brocaded Acorns was made in pink, white, ice green, ice blue, and vaseline.

BROCADED DAFFODILS

Like the other brocaded patterns, this was made by Fostoria. The shape is a 7½″ x 6½″ handled bowl in pink. The lovely pattern consists of beautifully realistic daffodils, leaf swirls, and small star fillers.

BROCADED PALMS

Shown is one example of Fostoria's Brocaded series, a large handled cake plate in Brocaded Palms pattern. As you can see, the design is created with an acid cutback effect on the glass before iridization and the edges are gold-trimmed. All the patterns are generally handled in this manner and colors found include ice green, ice blue, pink, white, and a lovely and rare rose shade, as well as a rare vaseline color.

Bouquet

Boutonniere

Heisey Breakfast Set

Brocaded Acorns

Brocaded Daffodils

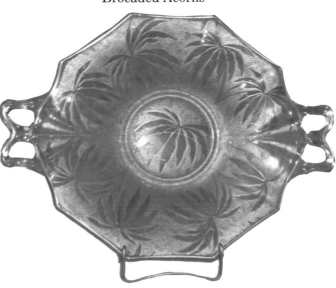

Brocaded Palms

BROKEN ARCHES

Broken Arches is a beautiful geometric Imperial pattern found only in punch sets of rather stately size. Not only is the coloring good, but the mold work is outstanding. The colors are marigold and amethyst. Often there is a silver sheen to the latter which detracts from its beauty, but when a set is found without this gun-metal look, the result is breathtaking. The marigold set is more common and sells for much less than amethyst. A green Broken Arches would be a great rarity.

BROOKLYN BOTTLE

I suspect this beautiful 9⅝″ cruet may be of European origin. The glass is very thin and the non-iridized handle and stopper are very attractive amethyst glass.

BROOKLYN BRIDGE

Like the Pony bowl pattern, this beautiful advertising bowl apparently came from the Dugan factory. The only color reported is marigold and the mold work is outstanding. Brooklyn Bridge is a scarce and desirable pattern.

BULLS EYE AND LEAVES

Confined to the exterior of bowls and found mostly in green or marigold, this pattern is a trifle too busy to be very effective and is certainly not one of Northwood's better efforts. All in all, there are five motifs, including leaves, beads, circles, fishnet, and a petal grouping. Although each appears on other Northwood products, not in this combination.

BUTTERFLIES

This outstanding Fenton pattern is found only on bon-bons often flattened into a card tray shape. The colors are very good with eight butterflies around the edges and one in the center. The exterior carries a typical wide panel pattern and often is found with advertising on the base. Colors are marigold, cobalt blue, green, amethyst, and white. At least these are the ones I've heard about.

BUTTERFLIES AND WARATAH

Normally seen in the compote shape, this one has been flattened into a very stylish footed cake stand. The beautiful purple is typical of Australian Carnival glass and can stand with the best. It is also found in marigold.

Broken Arches

Brooklyn Bottle

Brooklyn Bridge

Bulls Eye and Leaves

Butterflies

Butterflies and Waratah

BUTTERFLY

The only shape chosen for this Northwood pattern is the bon-bon and most of the ones I've seen are on amethyst base glass, although marigold and green are found occasionally and pastels have been reported. The pattern shows a lone butterfly in the center of a stippled rays pattern. Not too imaginative but the butterfly shows quite good detail.

BUTTERFLY TUMBLER

Shown is one of the most expensive glass tumblers known. This particular example brought more than $4000.00 in trade and cash a while back, which only proves scarcity plus desire equals big bucks. The Butterfly tumbler is on a pale amberish marigold. The edging design is much like Shell and Jewel, but Butterfly is a U.S. Glass product. A matching footed pitcher has been rumored but not confirmed.

BUTTERFLY AND BERRY

This is certainly one of the Fenton Company's prime designs and can be found on a large array of shapes, including footed berry sets, table sets, water sets, a footed hatpin holder, vases, a rare spittoon whimsey and a rare footed bowl whimsey. Colors are marigold, cobalt blue, green, amethyst, white, and rarely red.

BUTTERFLY AND CORN VASE

This interesting vase is rare for several reasons and it is a pleasure to show it here. First is the pattern which has been reported only twice in the past few years. Both examples are identical in size (5⅞" tall and 2¾" base diameter). Secondly, the base color of the glass is vaseline with a marigold finish. While this coloring is found rarely on both Millersburg and Northwood items, I believe the Butterfly and Corn vase to be a product of the latter.

BUTTERFLY AND FERN

For many years, collectors considered this very beautiful water set a Millersburg product and indeed the color and finish rival products of the Ohio Company, but Butterfly and Fern is a Fenton item for sure. The mold work is outstanding and the available colors of marigold, amethyst, green, and blue are marvelous!

BUTTERFLY AND TULIP

Make no mistake about it, this is a very impressive Dugan pattern. The bowl is large, the glass heavy and the mold work exceptional. Found in either marigold or purple, this footed jewel has the famous Feather Scroll for an exterior pattern. Typically, the shallower the bowl, the more money it brings, with the purple bringing many times the price of the underrated marigold.

Butterfly

Butterfly Tumbler

Butterfly and Berry

Butterfly and Corn Vase

Butterfly and Fern

Butterfly and Tulip

BUTTERFLY BOWER

The interior design of a stippled central butterfly flanked by trellis work and flora is hard to see, however, the exterior's S-Band pattern shows quite well. This deep bowl is 6½″ across and stands 3″ tall. It can be found in marigold and purple. The rim has a bullet edge. Manufactured in Australia.

BUTTERFLY ORNAMENT

I'm told this interesting bit of glass was made as a give-away item and attached to bon-bons, baskets and compotes by a bit of putty when purchasers visited the Fenton factory. This would certainly explain the scarcity of the Butterfly ornament for few are around today. Colors I've heard about are marigold, amethyst, cobalt blue, ice blue, white, and green.

BUTTERMILK GOBLET

Exactly like the Iris goblet also made by Fenton, the plainer Buttermilk Goblet is a real beauty and rather hard to find, especially in green or amethyst. As you can see, the iridescence is on the interior of the goblet only and the stem is the same as the Fenton Vintage compotes.

BUTTON AND DAISY HAT

Again, here is an item that has been reproduced in every type of glass known, but the example shown is old and original, and has resided in one of the major Carnival Glass collections in the country for many years. Like so many of the miniature novelty items, the coloring is a beautiful clambroth with lots of highlights. Manufacturer unknown.

BUZZ SAW CRUET

This eagerly hunted Cambridge novelty always brings top dollar when it comes up for sale. Found in two sizes, the colors seen are green and marigold. The mold work is fantastic as is the iridescence. Oddly, the base shows a pontil mark indicating the cruet was blown into a mold. Normally, the Buzz Saw Cruet was sold with a matching glass stopper, but the one shown (like so many around today) has long since lost the stopper. Again, these were probably designed as containers for some liquid, but just what, we can't say.

CANE

Known to be one of the older Imperial patterns, Cane is found on wine goblets, bowls of various sizes and pickle dishes. The coloring is nearly always a good, strong marigold, but the bowl has been seen on smoke and I'm sure amethyst is a possibility. Cane is not one of the more desirable Imperial patterns and is readily available, especially on bowls; however, a rare color would certainly improve the desirability of this pattern.

Butterfly Bower

S-Band Exterior

Butterfly Ornament

Button and Daisy Hat

Buzz Saw Cruet

Butterfly Goblet

Cane

CANE AND SCROLL

I'd guess there are other shapes around in this English pattern, but the small creamer shown is the only one I've seen so far. As you can see there are four busy patterns competing with one another but their combination isn't unattractive. The marigold has a reddish hue.

CANNON BALL VT.

While the shape of this Fenton water set is the same as the Cherry and Blossom usually found in cobalt, this marigold version has a much different enameled design. The tumblers have an interior wide panel design and I'm sure this is quite a scarce item.

CAPTIVE ROSE

Captive Rose is a very familiar decorative pattern found in bowls, bon-bons, compotes and occasional plates in colors of marigold, cobalt blue, green, amethyst, amber, and smoke. The design is a combination of embroidery circles, scales and diamond stitches and is a tribute to the mold maker's art. The roses are like finely stitched quilt work. Manufactured by Fenton.

CAROLINA DOGWOOD

This very interesting Fenton pattern is rather hard to find and the few examples I've seen have all been on milk glass base with either a marigold lustre or a beautiful bright aqua finish. The design is fairly good, featuring a series of six dogwood sprays around the bowl with a single blossom in the center. Simple but effective.

CARTWHEEL COMPOTE

Not only is this flash-iridized compote marked, it is marked twice — on the base and on the bowl. The color is pale as are most items from the Heisey Company, but quite pretty.

CATHEDRAL (CURVED STAR)

Shown is the British version of the Imperial Curved Star pattern. Shapes made in England are the chalice, a footed pitcher, footed creamer, covered butterdish in two sizes, a compote, a flower holder, and bowls of various sizes. Colors are marigold, blue, and amethyst. Cathedral is a product of Davisons of Gateshead.

Cane and Scroll

Cannon Ball Vt.

Captive Rose

Carolina Dogwood

Cartwheel Compote

Cathedral (Curved Star)

CHATELAINE

Most of the authorities in the field agree this very rare, beautiful water set pattern is an Imperial item. I'm listing it as a questionable one, however, because I've seen no proof of its origin. Of course I can't emphasize too strongly its quality or scarcity and the selling price on the few examples to be sold publicly verify this. The only color I've heard of is a deep rich purple.

CHECKERBOARD WATER SET

It has been pretty well established that the Checkerboard Water Set was a Westmoreland product, which partially explains its rarity today. I've seen about half a dozen tumblers over the years but the pitcher shown is one of only three known to exist. The color, iridescence and mold-work are outstanding.

CHERRY

Almost every carnival glass company produced one or more cherry patterns and for many years the Dugan Cherry was much confused with the Millersburg Cherry pattern. Of course, there is a considerable difference on comparison and much of the confusion has now been dispelled. The Dugan version is confined to bowls, flat or footed. It has fewer cherries on the branches, no stippling on the branches, and less detailed veining on the leaves. The exterior pattern (if there is one) is often Jeweled Heart.

CHERRY, MILLERSBURG

For many years, Northwood was credited with this beautiful pattern (much as the Fenton company had been for the "Poinsettia" bowl we now know was made by Northwood) but in recent years this error has been rectified. To be sure, the Northwood company did make two Cherry patterns but the Millersburg Cherry is easily distinguished from either of these, since it has more cherries in the clusters, greater variety in the leaf design and appears to be almost "drooping" in appearance.

Shapes: Water sets	Whimsey Banana Compote (very rare)
Table sets	Plate (very rare)
Berry sets	Compote (rare)
	Powder Jar (rare)

CHERRY AND CABLE

Sometimes called "Cherry and Thumbprint", this is a very difficult Northwood product to locate and to date I've seen one tumbler, one pitcher, a table set and a small berry bowl. The pattern is very much a typical Northwood design and reminds one of the famous Northwood Peach, especially in the shape of the butter dish bottom which carries the same exterior base pattern as the Prisms compote. I know of no colors except a good rich marigold, but others may certainly exist.

CHERRY CHAIN

Cherry Chain is a close relative of the Leaf Chain pattern shown elsewhere in this book. Found on bowls, plates and bon-bons, this all-over pattern is well done and effective. The colors are marigold, blue, green, amethyst, and white. I show an extremely rare example of this pattern on a red slag base glass and it is the only one I've heard about.

Chatelaine

Checkerboard Water Set

Cherry

Cherry, Millersburg

Cherry and Cable

Cherry Chain

CHERRY CIRCLES

This Fenton piece employs a pattern of fruit combined with a scales pattern, the latter being a favorite filler device at the Fenton factory. Cherry Circles is best known in large bon-bons, but compotes, bowls, and occasional plates do exist in marigold, cobalt blue, green, amethyst, and white.

CHRISTMAS COMPOTE

Some dispute has arisen over the origin of this large and beautiful compote and while some declare it a Millersburg product, I'm inclined to believe it came from the Northwood factory. It is rare and available in both purple and marigold.

CHRYSANTHEMUM

For years I thought this might be an Imperial pattern for it so reminded me of the Windmill pattern, but it really is Fenton. Found on large bowls, either footed or flat, Chrysanthemum is known in marigold, blue, green, ice green, white, and a very beautiful red.

CHRYSANTHEMUM DRAPE LAMP

This beauty would grace any glass collection. As you can see the font is beautifully iridized and has been found in pink glass as well as white. Strangely, most of these lamps have been found in Australia, but the maker is thus far unknown.

CIRCLE SCROLL

Dugan's Circle Scroll is not an easy pattern to find, especially in the water sets, hat shape, and vase whimseys. Other shapes known are berry sets, compotes, creamers, and spooners. The colors I've seen are marigold and purple, but certainly others may exist with cobalt a strong possibility.

CLASSIC ARTS

What an interesting pattern this is. It is available in a covered powder jar, a rosebowl, a 7″ celery vase, and a rare 10″ vase. The design is very "Greek" in feeling and the tiny figures quite clear. The green paint gives an antiquing effect which adds greatly to the beauty. Classic arts is a product of Davisons of Gateshead.

Cherry Circle

Chrysanthemum

Circle
Scroll

Christmas Compote

Chrysanthemum Drape Lamp

Classic Arts

43

CLEVELAND MEMORIAL TRAY

I'm very happy to be able to show this scarce Millersburg item in the vary rare marigold because few collectors have seen this pattern in anything but amethyst. Undoubtedly made to celebrate Cleveland's centennial birthday, this cigar ash tray depicts the statue of Garfield, his tomb in Lake View cemetery, the Soldiers and Sailors Monument, the Superior Street viaduct, and the Cleveland Chamber of Commerce building. The coloring and iridescence are typically Millersburg and the mold work compares favorably with that of the Courthouse bowl. A real treasure for any glass collector.

COBBLESTONES

This simple Imperial pattern is not often seen, but certainly is a nice item when encountered. Found on bowls of various sizes — often with Arcs as an exterior pattern, Cobblestones is also found on handled bonbons where a beautiful radium finish is often present and the exterior is honeycombed! A curious circumstance to say the least! The colors are marigold, green, blue, amethyst and amber.

COIN DOT

This pattern is fairly common on medium size bowls but can sometimes be found on rosebowls, plates, and a handled basket whimsey. The colors are marigold, cobalt blue, green, amethyst, and red but not all shapes are found in all colors and the bowl and rosebowl are the only shapes reported in red. Manufactured by Fenton.

COIN DOT ROSEBOWL

What a beauty this rare little rose bowl is! The glass is an aqua base with a very rich purple lustre. And while many people feel this is a Fenton product, I'm not completely sure who made it.

COIN SPOT

This undistinguished little Dugan compote holds a dear spot in my heart for it was the first piece of carnival glass we ever owned. Made in opalescent glass also, in carnival glass it is found in marigold, green, purple, peach, white, and blue. The design is simple, consisting of alternate rows of indented stippled ovals and plain flat panels. The stem is rather ornate with a finial placed mid-way down. Often in marigold, the stem remains clear glass.

COLONIAL

Imperial's Colonial pattern is simply one version of wide panelling. The shapes I've heard about are vases, toothpick holders, open sugars, candlesticks and the handled lemonade goblet shown. Colors are marigold, green and purple, usually of the very rich nature.

Cleveland Memorial Tray

Cobblestone

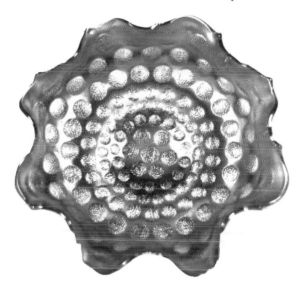

Coin Dot

Coin Dot Rosebowl

Coin Spot

Colonial

COLONIAL LADY

Just look at the color on this rare vase! It certainly rivals Tiffany and only proves Imperial was topped by no one in purple glass. Colonial Lady stands 5¾″ tall and has a base diameter of 2¾″. I've heard of no other color, except marigold, but certainly others may exist. Needless to say, these are not plentiful.

COLUMBIA

Made first in crystal, Columbia is found in Carnival Glass on compotes and vase shapes, all from the same mold. The coloring is usually marigold, but amethyst and green are known. While the simplicity of Columbia may not be appreciated by some collectors, it certainly had its place in the history of the glass field and should be awarded its just dues. Manufactured by Imperial.

CONCAVE DIAMOND

Most of us have seen the Concave Diamond water sets in ice blue and tumblers in vaseline, but I hadn't seen another shape until encountering this quite rare pickle caster in a beautiful marigold. That brought back a memory of finding a small fragment of this pattern in the Dugan shards from the 1975 Indiana, Pennsylvania, diggings, so I would speculate this rare item originated at that factory. Also known are "tumble-ups" in aqua, marigold and aqua opalescent.

CONCORD

Even among all the other grape patterns in iridized glass, I'm sure you won't confuse Concord with the others, for the netlike filler that covers the entire surface of the bowls' interior is unique. Found in both bowls and plates, Concord is a very scarce Fenton pattern and is available in marigold, green, amethyst, blue and amber. It is a collector's favorite and doesn't sell cheaply.

CONE AND TIE

The simple beauty of this very rare tumbler (no pitcher is known of now) is very obvious; and while most collectors credit it to Imperial, I can not verify its maker. The coloring is a very outstanding purple on the few examples known and the selling price only emphasizes its desirability. Rarely does one of these move from one collection to another.

CONSTELLATION

Constellation is a seldom seen compote, rather smaller than most. It measures 5″ tall and has a bowl diameter that averages 5½″ across. The exterior pattern is called Seafoam and I've seen this compote in peach opal, a strange white, over yellow (vaseline) glass and white Carnival. It was made by Dugan.

Colonial Lady

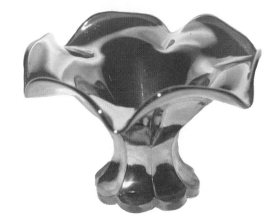

Columbia

Concave Diamond

Concord

Cone and Tie

Constellation

CORAL

I'd guess the same designer who gave us the Peter Rabbit and Little Fishes pattern is also responsible for Coral; the bordering device for all three is almost identical. Coral is found in bowls mostly, but a rare plate and a rarer compote are known in various colors, including marigold, blue, green, vaseline and white. Manufactured by Fenton.

CORINTH AND VT.

Long attributed to Northwood, Corinth is another pattern from the Dugan factory. It is found on bowls, vases and the beautiful banana dish shown, in marigold, green, amethyst, and peach opalescent. The example shown is 8¼" long and is iridized on the inside only.

CORN BOTTLE

Perhaps the Corn Bottle is not an Imperial product, but the beautiful helios green has always made me feel it was and so while I list it as a questionable Imperial product, I stand convinced it is. Colors found are marigold, green, amethyst, and smoke (another indication Imperial made it), all of good quality. The iridescence is usually outstanding as is the moldwork. It stands 5" tall and usually has a cork stopper.

CORN VASE

This is one of the better known Northwood patterns and that's little wonder because it is such a good one. Usually about 7" tall, there are certain variants known; especially noteworthy is the rare "pulled husk" variant that was made in very limited amounts. The colors are marigold, green, purple, ice blue, ice green, and white. The mold-work is outstanding, the color superior and the glass fine quality — truly a regal vase.

COSMOS

Green seems to have been the favorite color in this Millersburg pattern and small bowls abound; however, an occasional 7" plate can be found. The radium finish is spectacular and the mold work outstanding.

COSMOS AND CANE

Found in compotes, bowls, table sets, water sets, a tumbler with advertising, rosebowls, and a rare spittoon whimsey, Cosmos and Cane is one of those Imperial patterns that was later made in England by Sowerbys. The American version is found in white or clambroth in all shapes except the rosebowl, while the British version was made in marigold and a beautiful satiny purple.

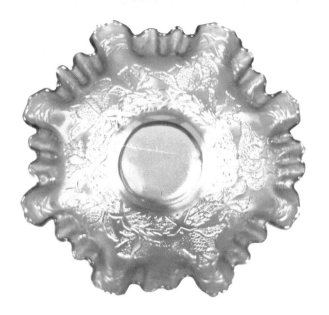

Coral

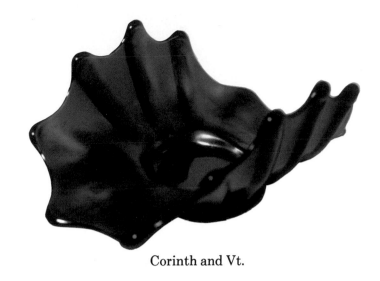

Corinth and Vt.

Corn Bottle

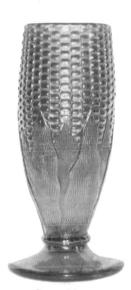

Corn Vase

Cosmos

Cosmos and Cane

COSMOS VT.

While this nicely patterned item has been confused with the Millersburg Cosmos pattern, I'm quite sure Cosmos Variant is a Fenton pattern found in bowls and occasionally plates (a compote has been reported but I haven't seen it.) Amethyst is probably the most available color but Cosmos Variant can be found in marigold, purple, blue, white, iridized milk glass, and red.

COUNTRY KITCHEN

Used as both a primary and secondary pattern this hard-to-come-by design is quite artistic. The berry sets are next to impossible to locate and the four piece table sets are quite scarce and expensive. These, of course, are all primary uses; however, Country Kitchen is more often seen as an exterior pattern on the lovely Fleur-de-lis bowls where it compliments the latter perfectly. Millersburg seemed to have a flair for creating outstanding near-cut patterns and this is certainly one of them.

Shapes:

Table Sets
Bowls
Spittoon Whimsey
Milk Pitcher

COURTHOUSE

Frankly, I wasn't greatly impressed by the first of these I saw. I'm not quite sure what I'd expected but perhaps it was the smallness of the bowl that disappointed me. Now, however, I wouldn't part with my Courthouse bowl and I find my admiration for it growing each time I look at it. Known in two shapes — plain or ruffled — and two variations — lettered or unlettered — this 7″ shallow bowl typifies the Millersburg technique. The mold work is sharp and detailed and the glass is very fine and transparent. These things, added to the radium finish, spell quality — a rare thing for a piece of souvenir glass, and points out the Frank Fenton flair for quality regardless of cost.

COVERED HEN

The Covered Hen is probably the best recognized piece of English Carnival glass, made at the Sowerby Works. Known in a good rich marigold as well as a weak cobalt blue, the Covered Hen is 6⅞″ long. The mold work is very good but the color ranges from very good to poor. While reproductions have been reported, my British sources tell me this isn't true and that no examples have been made since the 1940's.

COVERED SWAN

This beautiful English pattern is a companion to the Covered Hen and can be found in both marigold and amethyst. It measures 7¾″ long and as you can see the neck doesn't touch the back! What a mold maker's achievement! The base is identical to that of the Covered Hen dish.

CRAB CLAW

Crab Claw is indeed a curious near-cut pattern that very seldom enters discussions by collectors, but isn't as readily found as many other geometrics from the Imperial Company. Found on bowls of various sizes, a two piece fruit bowl and base, and scarce water sets, the pattern is most often found in marigold, but amethyst and green are known in the bowl shapes. The design features hobstars, curving file and diamond devices, and daisy-cut half-flowers, all seemingly interlocking.

Cosmos Vt.

Country Kitchen

Courthouse

Covered Hen

Covered Swan

Crab Claw

CRACKLE

Crackle is a very common, very plentiful pattern available in a large variety of shapes, including bowls, covered candy jars, water sets, auto vases, punch sets, plates, spittoons, and a rare window ledge planter. Marigold is certainly the most found color, but green and amethyst do exist on some shapes. And often the color and finish are only adequate. Crackle was mass produced in great amounts, probably as a premium for promotional giveaways, so I suppose we can't expect it to equal other Carnival items.

CRUCIFIX

Now known to be from the Imperial Glass Company, these rare candlesticks are known in marigold Carnival glass and crystal. The Crucifix candlestick is 9½″ tall and is very heavy glass.

CRYSTAL CUT

This beautiful compote comes to us from Australia and as you can see, is a very nice geometric design. Other colors and shapes may exist, but if so, I haven't seen them. It measures 7″ in diameter.

CURVED STAR

This pattern was made by both Imperial and Davisons of England and it is difficult to tell just what by each. We do know both bowls and compotes come from both factories and apparently the rare pitcher, chalice, flower holder, epergne, and creamers come from England. Colors are marigold, blue, green, and purple.

CUT COSMOS

How I wish I knew who made this beautiful tumbler! The design is top-notch and certainly deserves full recognition, but the maker remains unknown. The only color reported is marigold and no matching pitcher is known.

CUT FLOWERS

Here is one of the prettiest of all the Jenkins' patterns. Standing 10½″ tall, the intaglio work is deep and sharp and the cut petals show clear glass through the luster, giving a beautiful effect. Most Cut Flowers vases are rather light in color, but the one shown has a rich deep marigold finish. Cut Flowers can also be found in a smoke color.

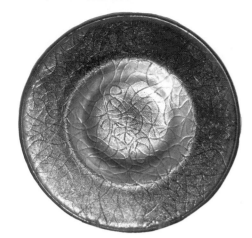

Crackle

Crucifix

Crystal Cut

Curved Star

Cut Cosmos

Cut Flowers

CUT OVALS

This Fenton pattern falls into the stretch glass field but, because of the etching, is considered carnival glass. Known in both candlesticks and bowls, Cut Ovals can be found in marigold, smoke, ice blue, ice green, pink, white, tangerine, lavender, red, and vaseline. The candlesticks are 8½″ tall and the bowls are known in 7″, 8″, 9″ and 10″ sizes.

DAHLIA

Make no mistake, Dahlia is an important, often scarce, always expensive, Dugan pattern. The glass is fine quality, the design highly raised and distinct, and the iridescence super. Found only in marigold, purple, and white, Dahlia is made only in berry sets, table sets, and water sets, all useful shapes, which probably explains the scarcity due to breakage in use. The water sets are much sought.

DAISY

Found only in the bon-bon shape, Fenton's Daisy pattern is seldom found. The pattern is a simple one of four strands of flowers and leaves around the bowl and one blossom with leaves in the center. While marigold has been reported, blue is the color most found and although I haven't seen amethyst or green they may exist.

DAISY AND CANE

This rare little decanter is a very unusual design, seldom seen. The coloring is typical of English marigold and has quite good iridescence. I've never seen the stopper so can't verify what it is like. The decanter stands 8″ tall and has a 3½″ base diameter. I suspect that Sowerby's made this, but can't say positively.

DAISY AND DRAPE

This pattern is probably a spin-off of the old U.S. Glass pattern, "Vermont", the main difference being the standing row of daisies around the top edge. Made in most of the Northwood colors, the purple leads the vivid colors, while aqua opalescent is the most sought of the pastels. White is probably the most available color, but even it brings top dollar.

DAISY AND PLUME

Daisy and Plume is an exterior pattern found on the large Northwood Blackberry compotes as well as the primary pattern of its own compotes and footed rosebowls. It is, of course, a very adaptable pattern and could be used on many shapes. One wonders why it does not appear on table sets or water sets, but unfortunately this is the case. The colors are marigold, white, purple, electric blue, green, peach, and aqua.

Dahlia

Cut Ovals

Daisy and Cane

Daisy

Daisy and Drape

Daisy and Plume

DAISY BASKET

Like many other of the Imperial handled baskets, in shape and size, the Daisy Basket is a large hat shaped one with one center handle that is rope patterned. The basket stands 10½″ tall to the handle's top and is 6″ across the lip. The colors are a good rich marigold and smoke, but be advised this is one of the shapes and patterns Imperial reproduced in the 1960's.

DAISY BLOCK ROWBOAT

Originally used as a pen tray in crystal, this Sowerby product had a matching stand, but I've never seen the stand in Carnival. Daisy Block was made in marigold, amethyst, and aqua in iridized glass. It measures 10½″ in length.

DAISY CUT BELL

What a joy this very scarce Fenton pattern is. It was called a "tea bell" in a 1914 catalog and as you can see, the handle is clear and scored and the Daisy design is all intaglio. The Daisy Cut Bell stands 6″ tall and is found in marigold only. It is a four mold design and has a marking inside "PATD APPLD".

DAISY SQUARES

Besides the very scarce stemmed rosebowl shown, this beautiful Millersburg pattern is found in a rare compote from the same mold. Colors are marigold, green, amber, and a lone amethyst. The interior has a honeycomb design.

DAISY WREATH

Apparently Mr. Fenton decided this pattern looked best on a milk glass base for I haven't heard of it any other way. The 9″ bowl shown is marigold on milk glass and is quite scarce. Equally scarce is the aqua blue on milk glass.

DANCE OF THE VEILS

I've heard of three of these beauties by the Fenton Company in iridized glass and they are truly a glassmaker's dream. Marigold is the only Carnival color although, crystal, pink, green, custard, and opalescent ones are made.

Daisy Basket

Daisy Block Rowboat

Daisy Cut Bell

Daisy Squares

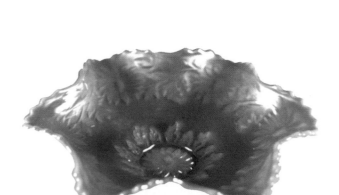

Daisy Wreath

Dance of the Veils

DANDELION

I have serious misgivings about labeling both of the pictured items as the same pattern, but since this is how they are best known, I will yield to tradition. Actually, the mug is certainly a dandelion pattern that is quite rare and popular, especially in aqua opalescent. Occasionally a mug bears advertising on the base and is called the "Knight Templar" mug; it brings top dollar!

The water set, while known as Dandelion, is not the same design, but nonetheless is an important Northwood pattern. It is found in marigold, purple, green, ice blue, white, and a very rare ice green. The tankard pitcher is regal.

DEEP GRAPE COMPOTE

Ever notice how few compotes were made by Millersburg? This is one of the rarer ones, found in cobalt, amethyst, green, marigold, and vaseline. It stands about 7″ high and the stem is panelled. The grape clusters and leaves are richly detailed and the mold work is outstanding.

DIAMOND AND DAISY CUT

This beautiful Jenkins pattern is found on 10″ vases, compotes, and rare water sets (which have been mistakenly labeled Mayflower). Found primarily in a good rich marigold, the compote has been seen in amethyst, so perhaps other colors exist.

DIAMOND AND FILE

I'm not at all sure this pattern is Imperial, but list it here as a possible one. It hasn't a great deal of imagination, but may have been intended give-aways or quick sales. The small bowl shown is quite deep, possibly intended as a jelly holder. The color is adequate and I've heard of these in smoke as well as marigold.

DIAMOND AND RIB

Diamond and Rib is a Fenton pattern that has caused great confusion in the collecting world. This is because the jardiniere shape was long suspected to be a Millersburg product. This size has been found in large vases just like the smaller ones, so that we know there were two sizes of molds used. Colors are marigold, green, amethyst, smoke, and blue.

DIAMOND AND SUNBURST

Known in bowls, decanters, goblets and the rare oil cruet shown, Diamond and Sunburst is an Imperial pattern. Colors are marigold, green, purple, and amber.

Deep Grape Compote

Dandelion

Diamond and Daisy Cut

Diamond and File

Diamond and Sunburst

Diamond and Rib

DIAMOND FLUTES

This English pattern is shown in a 7¼″ parfait glass. The coloring is a good marigold at the top, running to clear at the base. Other shapes are not reported, but may exist.

DIAMOND FOUNTAIN

This beautiful cruet has now been traced to the Higbee Company and appears in their 1910 ads as a pattern called Palm Leaf Fan in crystal. As you can see, the mold work is quite good and the color adequate.

DIAMOND LACE

There seems to be a great deal of doubt about the maker of this beautiful water set and some credit it to Imperial, while others proclaim it to be a Heisey product. I personally lean toward Imperial as the maker, because of the beautiful coloring, the mold sharpness and the clarity of glass. In most ways it greatly resembles the Chatelaine water set, or the Zippered Heart berry set as to coloring and mold work. Diamond Lace is found in berry sets and water sets in colors of marigold, and purple, but white has also been reported.

DIAMOND OVALS

Known in only two shapes thus far, a creamer on a foot and a stemmed compote, Diamond Ovals is a Sowerly product. The creamer is one of the smaller ones, measuring 4¾″ tall. The only color reported is marigold, but certainly others may exist.

DIAMOND PINWHEEL

Perhaps there are other shapes in this Davisons pattern, but if so, I haven't seen them. As you can see, it is a simple geometric design, but very pleasing. The glass and luster all have good quality and certainly add to any collection.

DIAMOND POINT

While this Northwood pattern is quite typical of most vase patterns, it has a certain distinction of its own. While refraining from "busyness", it manages an interesting overall pattern. It is found in purple, blue, green, marigold, peach, and white, and is normally of standard height, being 10″-11″ tall.

Diamond Flutes

Diamond Fountain

Diamond Lace

Diamond Ovals

Diamond Pinwheel

Diamond Point

DIAMOND POINT COLUMNS

I haven't heard of this Imperial pattern in any other color than a good rich marigold but that certainly doesn't mean they do not exist. The shapes known are compotes, plates, vases, table sets, and powder jars (which are rare). While the design of alternating rows of plain and checkered panels is quite simple, the overall appearance is quite effective.

DIAMOND POINTS BASKET

Although the dimensions are nearly the same as Northwood's Basket, the Diamond Points Basket is a much rarer pattern. And while some collectors have credited the Fenton Company with this much sought novelty, I lean toward Northwood as the maker. The colors found are marigold, purple, and a radiant cobalt blue. The mold work is sharp and precise and the iridescence heavy and outstanding. I have heard of less than a dozen of these baskets, so lucky are you if you own one.

DIAMOND PRISMS

Apparently the British loved compotes for here is yet another geometric design in that shape. I've seen this same compote shaped with the sides squared and it was also on the same shade of marigold with much amber in the tint.

DIAMOND RING

This typical geometric design of file fillers, diamonds, and scored rings is found on berry sets as well as a fruit bowl of larger dimensions. The usual colors of marigold and smoke are to be found and, in addition, the fruit bowl has been reported in a beautiful deep purple. While Diamond Ring is not an outstanding example of the glass maker's art, it certainly deserves its share of glory. Manufactured by Imperial.

DIAMONDS

Most collectors are familiar with this pattern in the water sets but it does appear on rare occasions in a punch bowl and base (no cups have yet come to light). Like its cousin, Banded Diamonds, the design is simple but effective. The glass and iridescence are very good and all have the "Millersburg look."

DIVING DOLPHINS

For many years this scarce item was credited to the Imperial Company, but we know now it was a Sowerly product. The interior carries the Scroll Embossed pattern and Diving Dolphins is found in marigold, blue, green, and amethyst with the latter easiest to find. It measures 7″ across the bowl and may be round, ruffled, turned in like a rosebowl, or five sided.

Diamond Point Columns

Diamond Points Basket

Diamond Prisms

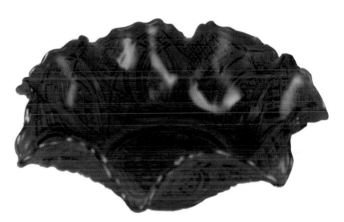

Diamond Ring

Diamonds

Diving Dolphins

DOGWOOD SPRAYS

This is a pattern so very familiar to all carnival collectors, for there are probably more bowls with various floral sprays than any other design. Dogwood Sprays, while well done, is not extraordinary in any sense of the word. Found on both bowls and compotes, the color most seen is peach but purple does turn up from time to time. Manufactured by Dugan.

DOLPHINS COMPOTE

If I had to pick my very favorite Millersburg pattern, this would be it — hands down. Not only is it unique in the entire field of carnival glass by virtue of its exterior design, but combined with the Rosalind interior, an almost perfect coordination is brought about. It simply looks good from any angle. Add to this the fine coloring and the radium finish and the Dolphins Compote is a true work of art, one that any company could be proud of.

DOUBLE DOLPHIN

Some people will probably question this pattern appearing here for it is rightly considered stretch glass, but the mold work of the dolphins tend to bridge the gap between stretch and Carnival Glass so I've shown it here. This Fenton pattern was made in many shapes, including bowls, compotes, vases, covered candy dishes, candlesticks and cake plates. Colors are ice blue, ice green, white, pink, red, topaz, tangerine and amethyst.

DOUBLE DUTCH

While it's difficult to say whether this pattern came before or after Windmill and the NuArt plate, it is quite obvious they were all the work of the same artist. All depict various rural scenes with trees, a pond, and bridge. This Imperial pattern is featured on a 9½" footed bowl, usually in marigold but occasionally found in smoke, green, and amethyst. The coloring is superior and the mold work very fine. The exterior bowl shape and pattern is much like the Floral and Optic pattern.

DOUBLE FAN TUMBLER (UNLISTED)

Please notice the very appealing shape of this rare, rare tumbler (two known), for it is very balanced as is the design. And while the coloring is only so-so, the glass is very clear and the mold work excellent. The Double Fan tumbler stands 3¾" tall and is 2½" across the diameter of the base. Certainly a complete water set would be a treasure indeed, regardless of the manufacturer.

DOUBLE LOOP

This Northwood pattern is found on creamers, as shown, and an open sugar with a stem. Often these are trademarked, but not all are. The colors known are marigold, green, purple, aqua opalescent, and cobalt, with the latter most difficult to find.

Dogwood Sprays

Dolphins Compote

Double Dolphin

Double Dutch

Double Fan Tumbler

Double Loop

DOUBLE SCROLL

The Double Scroll pattern was Imperial's try at an Art Deco pattern in iridized glass and can be found on candlesticks, a dome-based console bowl, and a punch cup in marigold, green, amethyst, smoke, and red (not all colors in all shapes). The candlesticks measure 8½" tall and the oval shaped console bowl that went with them is 10½" by 8½" in diameter and stands 5" tall. The scrolls are of solid glass. The glass is thick and fine and the coloring is excellent.

DOUBLE STAR

In reality,this is the same pattern as the Buzz Saw cruet, but for some reason it has been called by this different name. Found in water sets and a rare spittoon whimsey formed from a tumbler, this Cambridge pattern is seen mostly in green, but marigold and amethyst can be found. I consider Double Star one of the best designed water sets in all of Carnival glass.

DOUBLE STEM ROSE

Like other patterns made at the Dugan plant, this pattern has mistakenly been attributed to the Fenton Company. Double Stem Rose is found on dome-footed bowls of average size in marigold, blue, green, lavender, amethyst, and white. The design is interesting and well executed.

DRAGON AND BERRY (STRAWBERRY)

Obviously a companion piece to well-known Dragon and Lotus pattern, Dragon and Berry apparently didn't have the popularity of its cousin for few examples are to be found. Known in both footed and flat based bowls and in colors of marigold, green, and blue, this Fenton pattern is a much sought item.

DRAGON AND LOTUS

Probably one of the best known of all Carnival Glass patterns, Dragon and Lotus was a favorite of all Fenton patterns, produced over several years. Shapes are flat or footed bowls and rare plates. Colors are marigold, green, blue, amethyst, peach opalescent, iridized milk glass, aqua opalescent, vaseline opalescent, red and the pastels.

DRAGON'S TONGUE

Known mostly in light shades in a milk glass with marigold iridescence, Dragon's Tongue is also found on a large footed bowl that has a diameter measurement of 11". The only color reported on the bowl shape is marigold, but certainly other colors are possible, especially Fenton's famous cobalt blue.

Double Scroll

Double Star

Double Stem Rose

Dragon and Berry

Dragon and Lotus

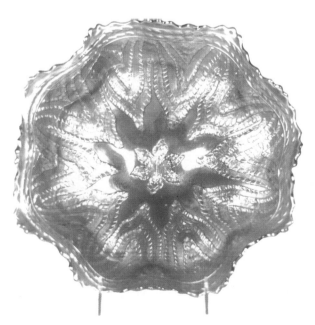

Dragon's Tongue

DRAPERY

This is a very graceful Northwood pattern, especially when the vase has been pulled out and down to form a lovely candy dish. One is instantly reminded of great folds of soft satin draperies in a theater, especially in the vase shape, most of which are 10″-11″ in height. The colors are marigold, peach, blue, purple, green, ice blue, and ice green.

ELKS

Found in bowls, plates and the quite rare bell shapes, the Fenton Elk pieces were produced to be sold at Elks conventions in Detroit (1910), Atlantic City (1911), and Parkersburg (1914). The colors found are a very rich cobalt blue and a sparkling emerald green with heavy lustre. Naturally the plates are more sought than the bowls and the bells are highly prized treasures.

ELKS, MILLERSBURG

The Millersburg Elks bowl or "two-eyed elk" is the best of all the elks bowls or plates. It is somewhat larger than the Fenton pieces. The only color I've seen is a rich amethyst with beautiful radium finish. In addition to plates, paperweights as well as a rare nappy have been found.

EMBROIDERED MUMS

Embroidered Mums is a rather busy pattern, saved from being overdone by a balancing of its parts. A close cousin to the Hearts and Flowers pattern, Embroidered Mums is found on bowls and bon-bons on a stem. Many of the pieces in this pattern carry the Thin Rib as a secondary pattern and perhaps a plate will someday be found. At least, it gives us something to hope for, because many Northwood patterns with this exterior are found in plates.

EMU

The Emu bowl is one of the better Australian patterns and is available on 4½″ and 10½″ bowls as well as large compotes and footed cake stands. The color most found is purple, but marigold and the amber over aqua base glass are found rarely. Some people call this pattern Ostrich, but the Ostrich lives in Africa and the Emu is an Australian bird with a similar appearance.

ENAMELED CARNIVAL GLASS

Toward the latter years of the Carnival glass "craze", patterns become simpler and in order to give the customer something different, items (especially water sets and bowls) were marketed with hand-painted enamel work on them. Most of these were simple floral sprays, but occasionally an interesting fruit pattern emerged, like the scarce water set shown here. Today, these seem to be gaining in popularity and certainly deserve a place in Carnival glass history. This is a Northwood pattern.

Drapery

Elks

Elks, Millersburg

Embroidered Mums

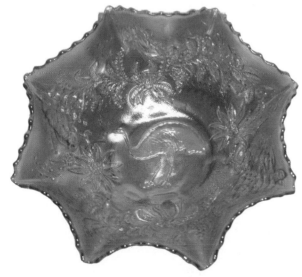

Emu

Enameled Carnival Glass

ENAMELED PRISM BAND

This beautiful Fenton tankard water set is a standout in the series of enameled water sets. It can be found in marigold, blue, green (rarely) and a very impressive and scarce white. Also the floral work may vary slightly from one item to another.

ENGLISH HOB AND BUTTON

This pattern has been reproduced in the last few years in this country, especially on tray and bowl shapes in an odd shade of amberish marigold on very poor glass. The English version shown is another thing however. The glass is clear and sparkling. The shapes are bowls, mostly, in marigold, green, amethyst, and blue.

ESTATE MUG

This rare little mug appears to belong in the late carnival era, but nevertheless is a much-in-demand item, especially to mug collectors. Most of these mugs are souvenir items and the one shown is no exception; it bears the inscription: "Souvenir of Gant, New York". The coloring is a pale marigold and the iridescence is only so-so. It measures 3″ tall.

FAN

Despite the fact most collectors have credited this pattern to Northwood, I'm really convinced it was a Dugan product. In custard glass it has been found with the well-known Diamond marking. Of course many more shapes of the Fan pattern were made in custard. In carnival glass, the availability is limited to the sauce dish and an occasional piece that is footed and has a handle.

The colors seen are marigold, peach, and purple. Peach is the most available color.

FAN-TAIL

Fan-Tail is a pattern found on occasion as the interior design of Butterfly and Berry bowls. Actually, the design is made up of a series of peacock's tails swirling out from the center of the bowl, and while it is an interesting pattern, certainly is not a designer's success.

This Fenton pattern has been reported in marigold, cobalt blue, green and white.

FANCIFUL

Probably many collectors will challenge this pattern being attributed to Dugan, but shards from the Dugan factory were identified by this author in both marigold and purple, so here it is. Actually, if a comparison is carefully made with the Embroidered Mums, Heart and Flowers and Fancy patterns, one finds a close similarity that isn't evident on first glance. Fanciful is available on bowls and plates in colors of marigold, peach, purple, and white. The familiar Big Basketweave adorns the exterior.

Enameled Prism Band

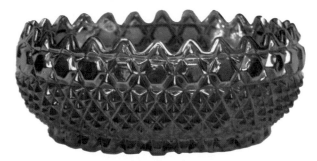

English Hob and Button

Estate Mug

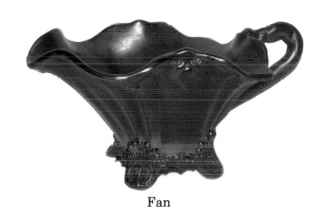

Fan

Fan-Tail

Fanciful

FANS

The most striking thing about this pitcher is its size; larger than a creamer but smaller than a milk pitcher. It stands 5″ tall and 7″ across the handle. The design is a series of prisms in fan shapes and the only reported color is marigold. I suspect Davisons is the maker.

FARMYARD

Most people have long felt this to be Harry Northwood's masterpiece, but with the discovery of peach opalescent and evidence that the exterior pattern (Jewelled Heart) is Dugan, Farmyard is likely to be from that company. Colors are purple, fiery amethyst, green, and peach opalescent.

FASHION

Fashion is probably the most familiar geometric pattern in all of Carnival Glass. It was manufactured in huge amounts over a long period of time and was originally called "402½" when first issued. The shapes are creamers, sugars, punch sets, water sets, a bride's basket, and a fruit bowl and stand. While marigold is the most often seen color, smoke, green and purple are found but are scarce. This pattern was made by Imperial.

FEATHER STITCH

This pattern is a kissing cousin of the well-known Coin Dot design and as such is found on bowl shapes only, although I suspect a plate shape does exist. The colors seen are marigold, blue, green and amethyst and the bowls may vary in size from 8½″ to 10″. Feather Stitch was produced by Fenton.

FEATHER AND HEART

This fine Millersburg water set, found in green, marigold, and amethyst is typical in many ways of all the Millersburg water sets. The pitcher lip is long and pulled quite low while the rim is scalloped quite like its cousin, the Marilyn set. The glass is quite clear, rather heavy and has excellent iridescence. A little difficult to find, the pattern adds greatly to any collection.

FEATHERED FLOWERS

This pretty exterior pattern is found on the Australian Kiwi bowls. It is an intaglio pattern of swirls and stylized blossoms and is quite attractive.

Fans

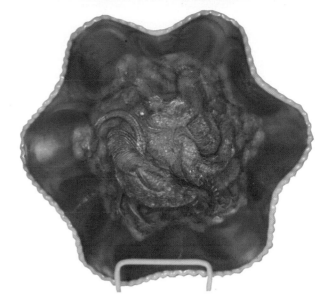

Farmyard

Fashion

Feather Stitch

Feather and Heart

Feathered Flowers

FEATHERED SERPENT

At one time, this pattern was felt to be a Millersburg design, but in recent years the Fenton Company has emerged as the known manufacturer. Found only in berry sets and a very rare spittoon whimsey, Feathered Serpent is available in marigold, green, blue, and amethyst and has the Honeycomb and Clover as an exterior pattern.

FEATHERS

Northwood certainly made its share of vases perhaps because they were so decorative and useful. The Feathers vase is an average example usually found in marigold, purple and green and is of average size and quality.

FENTONIA

Known in berry sets, table sets, fruitbowls, and water sets, Fentonia is an interesting all-over pattern of diamonds filled with the usual Fenton fillers of scales and embroidery stitchery. Colors are marigold, blue, green, and occasionally amethyst, but the pattern is scarce in all colors and is seldom found for sale. There is a variant called Fentonia Fruit.

FERN

Again we find a pattern that is sometimes combined with the well-known Northwood pattern, Daisy and Plume. Fern is usually found as an interior pattern on bowls and compotes. It is an attractive pattern but really not an outstanding one.

FERN PANELS

Like so many of the Fenton novelty pieces of Carnival Glass, Fern Panels is found only on the hat shape. Not too exciting, but then it apparently had an appeal of its own then as now. The colors are the usual ones: marigold, blue, green, and occasionally red.

FIELD FLOWER

Originally called "494½", this much overlooked Imperial pattern is really a little jewel. Found only on a standard size water set and a rare milk pitcher, Field Flower is found in marigold, purple, green, and a very beautiful clambroth. The design, basically a flower framed by two strands of wheat on a stippled background, is bordered by double arches that edge the stippled area and continue down to divide the area into panels. All in all, this is a beautiful pattern that would grace any collection.

Feathered Serpent

Feathers

Fentonia

Fern

Fern Panels

Field Flower

FIELD THISTLE

Field Thistle is a U.S. Glass Company pattern, scarce in all shapes and colors. Shapes known are berry sets, table sets, water sets, a vase, plate, and small creamer and sugar called a breakfast set. Colors most found are marigold or green, but the breakfast set is known in a beautiful ice blue so other colors may exist. The pattern is all intaglio and sometimes the marigold coloring is a bit weak.

FILE

For many years, File was designated as a product of the Columbia Glass Company, but was actually made by the Imperial Glass Company and is shown as such in their old catalogs in many shapes, including bowls, water pitchers, compotes and table sets. The colors are marigold, green, smoke, and amethyst and usually the lustre is quite good with much gold in evidence. The mold work is far above average.

FINE CUT AND ROSES

The real pleasure of this Northwood pattern is the successful combination of a realistic floral pattern with a pleasing geometric one. Of course rosebowls have a charm all their own. Really well done mold-work and super color all add to its attraction and even though it is slightly smaller than many rosebowl patterns, it is a favorite of collectors.

FINE PRISMS AND DIAMONDS

This large English vase stands some 13½" tall and has a hefty base diameter of nearly 4". Obviously it was intended to be used and not just a decorative item. And while the design qualities aren't impressive, the glass is of good color and luster.

FINE RIB

Can you imagine anything simpler? Yet the Fine Rib pattern was and is a success to the extent it was used time and time again by the Northwood company as secondary patterns and is the primary one in attractive vases like the one shown. While common in marigold and purple, the green color is a scarce one in Fine Rib.

FINE RIB VASE

While both Northwood and Fenton produced a Fine Rib vase pattern, there are differences in the design. On the Northwood vase, the ribbing extends all the way down on the base, while the Fenton design ends in a distinctive scalloped edge above the base. Of course Fenton made this shape and pattern in red too.

Field Thistle

File

Fine Cut and Roses

Fine Prisms and Diamonds

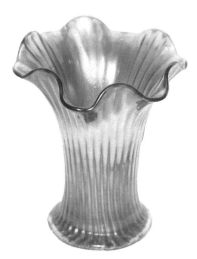

Fine Rib

Fine Rib Vase

FINECUT RINGS

From a set of copy-right drawings we know this pattern was made by the Guggenheim, Ltd.; Company of London in 1925. Shapes shown in the drawing, are an oval bowl, vase, footed celery, covered butterdish, creamer, stemmed sugar, round bowl, footed cake plate, and covered jam jar. The only color I've seen is marigold, and as you can see, the coloring, mold work, and luster are outstanding.

FISH VASE

Much like the Hand vase, this unusual design is listed here as a possible English pattern (I suspect it is a product of a French glass maker). It is marked "JAIN" and as you can see has a clear frosted area. The colors I've heard about are marigold, green, and amethyst.

FISHERMAN'S MUG

While I'm not completely convinced this is a Dugan pattern, it seems to be by a process of elimination. At any rate it is much sought and like the rarer Heron Mug, has the pattern on one side only. Colors are purple, amethyst, marigold, a rare peach opalescent, and a rarer blue.

FIVE HEARTS

Like so many of the Dugan patterns in peach opalescent, Five Hearts is found only on dome footed bowls of average size. It has been estimated that some sixty to seventy-five percent of all peach carnival was made by this company; personally, I'd say it would be closer to ninety percent.

FLEUR DE LIS

Named, of course, for the stylized figures which symbolize the lily of the French royal family, this beautiful Millersburg design is found on bowls of all shapes and as an interior pattern on an occasional Hobstar and Feather punch bowl. The overall pattern is formal though well-balanced and the quality of workmanship, iridescence and color rank with the best. Especially beautiful is the dome-footed three cornered bowl in amethyst.

FLEUR DE LIS VASE

Like other Jenkins patterns, this heavy vase has a deeply intaglio pattern. It stands a stately 10½" tall and is found on a rich marigold.

Finecut Rings

Fish Vase

Fisherman's Mug

Five Hearts

Fleur De Lis

Fleur De Lis Vase

FLORAL AND GRAPE

Without question, Floral and Grape is one of the most familiar of Fenton patterns for the water sets are plentiful, especially in marigold. The only other shape is a hat whimsey pulled from the tumbler and other colors are cobalt blue, amethyst, green, and a scarce white. Also, there are variations due to the wear of molds and creation of new ones. A variant is credited to the Dugan Company.

FLORAL AND OPTIC

Most people are familiar with this pattern in rather large footed bowls in marigold or clear Carnival, although it exists on rare cake plates and rose bowls, and in smoke, iridized milk glass, red, a stunning aqua Carnival Glass (shown) white, and iridized custard glass. The pattern is quite simple, a series of wide panels edged by a border band of vining flower and leaf design. A green or amethyst bowl in Floral and Optic would be a real find in this Imperial pattern.

FLOWER BLOCK

This English pattern is a spin-off of the Curved Star pattern and I'm showing it here in its entirety so collectors will be able to see the complete block as designed. Most of the ones around have lost their fancy wire base and wire arranger on the top.

FLOWER POT (BLUE)

While both Imperial and Fenton made these flower pot and saucer planters, the one shown is from the Fenton Art Glass Company. It is a beautiful ice blue and is 5″ tall and 4¾″ in diameter. The plate is 6¼″ in diameter. It has been seen mostly on pastels including pink but can also be found on marigold.

FLOWERING DILL

Once again we encounter a Fenton pattern that was chosen for the hat shape only, but Flowering Dill has a bit more to offer than some in that the design is graceful, flowing and covers much of the allowed space. Flowering Dill can be found in marigold, cobalt blue, green, and red.

FLOWERING VINE

The Flowering Vine compote is indeed a very scarce Millersburg item. To date, I've heard of only two examples, one in green and one in amethyst. The compote is a large one, some 9 inches high and 6½ inches across. The interior pattern is one of grape-like leaves and a dahlia-like flower. The finish is a fine radium one on heavy glass.

Floral and Grape

Floral and Optic

Flower Block

Flower Pot

Flowering Dill

Flowering Vine

FLOWERS AND FRAMES

Here is another of Dugan's dome-footed bowls found primarily in peach opalescent, but also available in marigold as well as purple and green. The bowls vary from 8″ to 10″ depending on the crimping of the rim and usually have very sharp mold detail.

FLUFFY PEACOCK

Once thought to be a Millersburg product (its really that pretty), Fluffy Peacock is now recognized as a Fenton product and as such is high on the list of their best in iridized glass. Known only in water sets, Fluffy Peacock is not too difficult to find in green or marigold; however, the beautiful cobalt blue is quite scarce and the amethyst is much sought.

MILLERSBURG FLUTE

The Millersburg Flute has one or two distinct differences from any of the other Flute patterns. One of course is the clarity of the base glass itself but the most pronounced is the ending of the flutes themselves plus the sixteen rays on the base. It is found in punch sets, berry sets and vases.

FLUTE

While it is certainly true all of the major makers of carnival glass used the Flute pattern in one way or another, apparently only Imperial and Northwood thought enough of it to make it a primary pattern. Thus we find many useful shapes in an array of colors coming from the Northwood factories — including sherbets, water sets, table sets, berry sets, and even individual salt dips (an item seldom encountered in carnival glass). The green water set is probably the rarest color and shape in this pattern.

FLUTE #3

After I wrote the Millersburg book, a great controversy arose around the Flute pattern I showed in a small bowl and punch set. Many people thought this was the Imperial pattern called Flute #3 (it wasn't), which I've seen only on table sets, water sets, a celery or large spooner, a small toothpick holder, a sauce bowl, a two handled toothpick holder, and a different punch set (since then I've seen a very large berry bowl). The obvious difference between these two Flutes is the bottom configuration. On the Imperial version, there is a definite hexagonal effect just above the base, while the Millersburg version is either slightly curved outward in a honeycomb effect or has a curved slope from the base upward.

FLUTE SHERBET

This little cutie is the only pattern in British glass I ever found with a marking and these are signed "BRITISH" in script on the underside of the base. In size they are small, measuring 3¼″ tall and 3″ across the top. The only color reported is a good marigold of deep hue.

Flowers and Frames

Fluffy Peacock

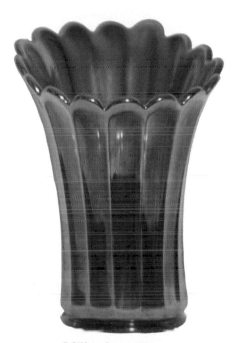

Millersburg Flute

Flute

Flute #3

Flute Sherbet

FLUTED SCROLLS FOOTED ROSEBOWL (AMETHYST)

Perhaps this should be called a spittoon, but regardless of the name it is a very rare, one-of-a-kind product in Carnival. While often found on opalescent glass, this is the only iridized item in this pattern I've heard of. Perhaps it was a novelty a Dugan worker produced for himself. The coloring is a good amethyst with average lustre.

FOOTED PRISM PANELS

What a nice design this pretty 10″ footed vase is! It is a Sowerly product and the only reported colors are a good rich marigold and a scarce green. The design is a series of six panels filled with star prisms in graduating sizes. The stem base is domed and gently scalloped, giving great grace to the appearance.

FOOTED SHELL

Made in two sizes, a 5″ and a 3″ size, this little novelty from the Westmoreland Company is a scarce item, especially in the smaller size. The shell rests on three stubby feet and the iridization is on the inside only. Colors I've seen are amethyst, green, marigold, and blue.

FORKS

I first showed this rare cracker jar in my Rarities book as an unlisted pattern but have since learned it was called "Forks" in old Cambridge ads. The only color I've seen is a very rich green, but I wouldn't rule out marigold or amethyst.

FORMAL

I'm a wee bit skeptical about this pattern, but new evidence points to Dugan as the maker. Nevertheless, it is an interesting pattern found only on the vase shaped in a jack-in-the-pulpit manner and a quite scarce hatpin holder. The colors most seen are purple and marigold, but I'm told pastels do exist. The hatpin holder stands 7¼″ tall.

FOUR FLOWERS AND VTS

For many years I've been puzzled by the origin of this beautiful design, but since peach opalescent is a prominent color, I'm satisfied it was also a Dugan product. Known in bowls and plates from 6″-11″, colors are purple, aqua, green, marigold, peach, blue, and smoke.

Fluted Scrolls Footed Rosebowl

Footed Prism Panels

Footed Shell

Forks

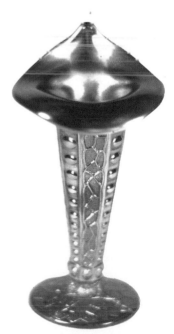

Formal

Four Flowers and Vts

474

Here is a very pretty near cut pattern that really looks quite good on all shapes. I know of punch sets, table sets, water sets and a milk pitcher in 474, as well as a nice fluted bowl. The color is usually marigold but amethyst and green do exist in some shapes, and are highly prized. The glass is heavy and clear, the coloring extra fine and the mold work superior; all making Imperial's 474 a real treat to own.

FRENCH KNOTS

I suppose most people credit this pattern to Fenton because of the shape — a typical hat with ruffled top. The design is quite nice, however, and gracefully covers most of the space except the base. The exterior is plain but nicely iridized and the only colors I've heard about are marigold and blue. French Knots is 4″ tall and has a base diameter of 2½″.

FROLICKING BEARS

Rare is hardly the word for this distinguished pattern and I certainly wish I could identify the maker positively, but I can't (although I lean toward the Fenton Company). The coloring is an odd gun metal luster over an olive green glass. The mold work is good, but not exceptional.

To date the Frolicking Bears tumbler has sold for more money than any other and the pitchers rank near the top of the market.

FROSTED BLOCK

Frosted Block is a very nice Imperial pattern found in several shapes including bowls, creamers, sugars, compotes, plates, milk pitchers, pickle dishes, and rosebowls. The color most seen is a good even marigold, but as you can see from the photo, a beautiful fiery clambroth is known in most shapes. In additon, some pieces are marked "Made in USA". These pieces are much scarcer and are well worth looking for.

FRUIT AND FLOWERS

Apparently a very close relative to the Three Fruits pattern, this is another of Northwood's floral groupings so well designed and produced. Also there are several variations of this pattern, some with more flowers intermingled with the apples, pears, and cherries, often meandering almost to the very outer edge of the glass. Again the Northwood Basketweave is the exterior pattern and Fruits and Flowers is found on compotes with handles as well as bowls.

MILLERSBURG FRUIT BASKET

I couldn't quite believe my eyes when I first saw this Millersburg compote. But, there it was with the exterior design and shape exactly like the Roses and Fruit Compote with an interior basketweave design and a pineapple, grapes and fruit! It was a real find and I've been grateful ever since for the privilege of photographing it. It is my belief that this compote was the original pattern design but had to be modified because of the difficulty in producing the intricate design and remain in a competitive price area. At this time four have been found. Of course, it must be classified as an extreme rarity.

474

French Knots

Frolicking Bears

Frosted Block

Fruits and Flowers

Millersburg Fruit Basket

FRUIT SALAD

While most authorities consider this to be a Fenton pattern, I very much feel it came from the Dugan factory. Known in both large and medium size punch sets, the colors are marigold, amethyst, and peach opalescent.

GARDEN PATH

Both the regular Garden Path and the variant will surprise many people appearing here but apparently they are Dugan patterns since I have catalogued a large chunk of a peach bowl from the Dugan diggings. The exterior pattern is Soda Gold, a pattern long believed to be an Imperial Glass pattern, but again let us emphasize "if it comes in peach carnival, it is probably Dugan." The 11″ Garden Path plate is one of the more renowned pieces of carnival glass and has sold for prices in excess of $4000.00.

GARLAND

Quite often you'll spot one of these nicely done footed rosebowls in cobalt blue or marigold, but the green is quite rare and I haven't heard of an amethyst one but I suspect it was made in that color. Made around 1911, these are shown in Fenton ads well up into the later days of iridized glass and must have been quite popular. There are three sets of wreaths and drapery around the heavily stippled bowl.

GAY 90's

Not only because of its extreme rarity but because the design is so very well suited for a water set is this pattern recognized as one of two or three top water sets in all of Carnival glass. In every regard, excellence of workmanship is obvious. Even the solid glass handle shows leaf veining at the top and intricate petal sliping at the base. Add to this the beautiful Millersburg finish and the clarity of superior glass and you have a real winner — the Gay 90's water set.

GODDESS OF HARVEST

Goddess of Harvest is the rarest of all Fenton bowl patterns and certainly deserves all the attention it gets. I've heard of six or seven of these beauties in colors of marigold, blue, and amethyst and each is highly treasured by its owner. The bowl measures about 9″ in diameter and is usually found with a candy ribbon edge.

GOLDEN CUPID

This very scarce Australian beauty is something to behold. In size it is only 5¼″ in diameter and quite shallow. The glass is clear with the cupid in gilt and a strong iridescence over the surface. It may be an ash tray, but I can't be sure. Large bowls are reported also.

Fruit Salad

Garden Path

Garland

Gay 90's

Goddess of Harvest

Golden Cupid

GOLDEN GRAPE

Known only in bowls or rose bowls on a collar base, this is a neatly molded item without much elaboration. The exterior is completely plain and the only colors found are marigold or pastel marigold, usually with a satin finish. Golden Grape was manufactured by Dugan.

GOLDEN HARVEST

Here is another U.S. Glass pattern found mostly in marigold but occasionally seen in amethyst and reported in white. As you will notice, the wines are different from the decanter but are the proper ones and the stopper is solid glass.

GOLDEN HONEYCOMB

This interesting Imperial pattern provides an all over design without being busy. The small bowls have odd little solid glass handles that are like the ones on the breakfast set while the plate and compote do not. The only color I've heard of is a good deep marigold with very rich iridescence. While this certainly isn't in the same class as the Dugan Honeycomb rosebowl, it is a better than average item to own.

GOLDEN WEDDING

I'm very pleased to show the complete item, just as sold. Notice that the cap is still sealed, the whiskey is still inside, the labels are intact and the beautiful box, dated December 31, 1924, gives us a time frame for the bottle. Several sizes exist from a full quart down to the tiny 1/10 pint size.

GOOD LUCK

I'm very sure every carnival glass collector is familiar with this pattern since most of us have found a place for an example in our collections at one time or another. The example shown is quite unusual in that it is a true aqua blue with reddish iridescence. It is the only example I've ever seen in this exact color although the Good Luck bowls and plates are found in a very wide range of colors. This piece was made by Northwood.

GRACEFUL

Once again we find a very simple pattern, so very different from most Northwood offerings in the carnival glass field. Found mostly on marigold, occasionally a rich purple or deep emerald green vase in this pattern will surface and when one of these is found, the simple beauty of the Graceful pattern becomes obvious.

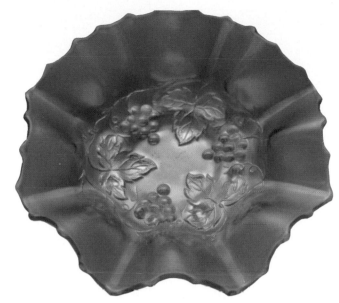

Golden Grape

Golden Harvest

Golden Honeycomb

Golden Wedding

Good Luck

Graceful

GRAPE, IMPERIAL

Perhaps reproductions have detracted too much from this beautiful Imperial pattern for most of us, but regardless of that, it remains a beautifully designed, nicely done pattern. In fact, for sheer realism, it doesn't take a backseat to any Grape pattern! The shapes are almost endless and the colors range from marigold to amethyst, green, smoke, clambroth and amber, all usually with a very fine lustre.

GRAPE AND CABLE

Yes, Fenton made a Grape and Cable pattern and it is often hard to distinguish it from Northwood's. Fenton's contribution is found in bowls (both flat and footed), plates, and large orange bowls usually with the Persian Medallion interior. Colors are marigold, green, amethyst, blue and rarely red.

GRAPE (AND CABLE)

Northwood Grape is, without question, the all-time favorite in carnival glass. Not only did it lead the field sixty years ago, it still does today. The variety of shapes available is staggering and the color availability large; the pastels are especially sought. Of course this pattern usually brings top dollar, especially in the rare shapes and colors. A small spittoon recently sold for $7000.00 at the Wishard auction. Whatever the undeniable appeal, this uncomplicated pattern has to be rated as the top item and entire collections of Grape aren't uncommon.

GRAPE AND CHERRY

Known only on large bowls, this Sowerly pattern is a real beauty. The design is exterior and all intaglio and is a series of grapes and cherries separated by an unusual torch and scroll design. The base has a grape and leaf design; also intaglio. The only colors I've heard about are marigold and cobalt blue but others may certainly exist.

GRAPE AND GOTHIC ARCHES

Made in a variety of kinds of glass including crystal, custard, gold decorated, and carnival glass, this pattern is certainly one of the earlier grape patterns. The arches are very effective, reminding one of a lacy arbor framing the grapes and leaves. While the berry sets often go unnoticed, the water sets are very desirable and are a must for all Northwood collectors.

GRAPE ARBOR

This is an underrated Northwood pattern, especially in the large footed bowl shape which carries the same exterior pattern as the Butterfly and Tulip. Of course the tankard water set is popular, especially in the pastel colors of ice blue, ice green, and white. The marigold set seldom brings top dollar and this is a shame for it is quite nice. The only other shape in Grape Arbor is a scarce hat shape.

Grape, Imperial

Grape and Cable

Grape (and Cable)

Grape and Cherry

Grape and Gothic Arches

Grape Arbor

GRAPE DELIGHT

Here is a pattern I'm sure will bring on a few outcries, because I've often heard it declared to be a Fenton product. I'm very sure, however, that it came from the Dugan family. On close comparison with several Dugan products, the mold-work is certainly compatible. Not only does it come in the scarce nut bowl shape shown but in the more often seen rosebowl. The colors are both vivid and pastel and the most unusual feature, the six stubby feet.

GRAPE LEAVES

Here is something really unusual — a marigold finish over a vaseline base glass. Of course, here we have another variation of a grape and leaf pattern that somewhat resembles both the Grape Wreath and Strawberry patterns discussed elsewhere in this book. The shape of the bowl is particularly noteworthy since it has no scalloping whatsoever. This pattern is a Millersburg product.

GRAPE LEAVES

Harry Northwood must have loved this pattern, for I've never seen a poor example. The purple bowls are, almost without exception, vividly brilliant with strong color and iridescence. The ice blue is one of the prettiest items in this color I've seen and green has also been found. It is sad no other shape was chosen for the Grape Leaves pattern, but this is the case. The exterior is the familiar Wild Rose pattern with a finely stippled background.

GRAPE WREATH

This bowl might be called the "missing link" for it stands squarely between the Blackberry Wreath and the Millersburg Strawberry and seems to be a part of the series — perhaps from the same designer.

Besides the various sizes of bowls, a rare spittoon whimsey, 6″ and 10″ plates are known.

GRAPEVINE LATTICE

I personally doubt the plate shown is really the same pattern as the water set known by the same name, but will give in to tradition and list them as one and the same. The plate and bowl could be called "Twigs" since they closely resemble the Apple Blossom Twigs pattern minus the flowers and leaves. The colors are both vivid and pastels, usually with very good iridescence. This pattern was manufactured by Dugan.

GREEK KEY

This simple continuous Northwood pattern, called Roman Key in pressed glass, is really very attractive when iridized. Actually, there are three motifs used; the Ray central pattern, the Greek Key and the Beads (in the much sought water set a fourth motif of prisms is added). Besides the water set there are flat and footed bowls as well as plates. The colors are both vivid and pastels.

Grape Delight

Grape Leaves

Grape Leaves

Grape Wreath

Grapevine Lattice

Greek Key

HAMMERED BELL

Whoever made this scarce and attractive light shade should be most proud for it is an imaginative work of art. Found only on a frosty white, the pattern is clear and distinct. The metal handle may vary in design but all were used to suspend the bell **above** or **below** the bulb.

HARVEST FLOWER

What a beauty this scarce water set pattern is! In design and mold work it is much like Dugan's Vineyard design but I can not say with certainty it came from that company. The entire surface is patterned which adds so much to the appearance. The tumbler has been reported in amethyst.

HATTIE

While there is little to be called outstanding about Hattie it, nonetheless, has its own charm and has the distinction of having the same pattern on both the exterior and interior. Most often found on 8" bowls with a collar base, it is also found in a scarce rose bowl and two sizes of plates, both of which are rare. The color most seen on this Imperial product is marigold, but green and amethyst do exist and I've heard of both amber and smoke bowls.

HEAVY GRAPE

Once called a Fenton product, this beautiful Grape design is now known to be an Imperial pattern and is available on berry sets, nappies, custard sets and plates in three sizes. The colors on most pieces are simply spectacular and include marigold, green, purple, smoke, amber, pastel green, smokey blue, and clambroth. The 11" chop plate is highly sought and always brings top dollar when sold.

HEADDRESS

This pattern was turned out by both the Imperial Glass Company and Sowerby's of England and it is very difficult to tell just who made what. However, I am fairly confident that some of the compotes and most of the bowls are Imperial. The design is very clean and the color usually top notch.

HEART AND HORSESHOE

Yes, Fenton had a version of the Good Luck pattern and it is much harder to find than the one Northwood produced. Note that it is simply the familiar Heart and Vine pattern with the horseshoe and lettering added. Colors are marigold and green with the marigold most prevalent and the green very hard to find.

Hammered Bell

Harvest Flower

Hattie

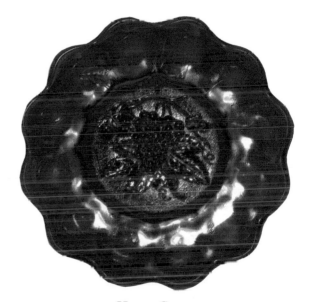

Heavy Grape

Headdress

Heart and Horseshoe

HEART AND TREES

Found as an interior pattern on some of the footed Butterfly and Berry bowls, Heart and Trees is a combination of three well known Fenton standards. Colors known are marigold, green, and blue but certainly others may exist.

HEART AND VINE

Apparently this was one of Mr. Fenton's favorite designs, for he used several variations of it combined with the Butterfly and Berry pattern as Stream of Hearts or on the Heart and Horseshoe pattern. The Heart and Vine pattern can be found on both bowls and plates and occasionally with advertising on the latter (the Spector plate). Colors are marigold, green, amethyst, blue and white.

HEARTS AND FLOWERS

Hearts and Flowers is an intricate pattern, like so many others favored by the Northwood company. It is found on various sizes and shapes of bowls as well as small, very graceful compotes. Apparently it was designed as a close relative of the Fanciful and Embroidered Mums patterns, perhaps by the same mold-maker. Interestingly enough, the compotes in the pattern are very similar in shape to the Persian Medallion compotes attributed to the Fenton Glass Company.

HEAVY BANDED DIAMONDS

Perhaps designed as a companion to the Banded Diamonds water set, this beautiful Australian berry set, available in both marigold and purple, is a joy to behold. The diamonds are heavily molded and stand out below the narrow thread lines and the iridescence is very rich.

HEAVY DIAMOND

I'd always thought this pattern to be a Dugan product until this vase shape in smoke appeared, so apparently it is an Imperial product. Previously reported only in marigold, shapes known besides the vase are large bowls, creamers and sugars, but others probably are around.

HEAVY GRAPE

So similar in many ways to the Millersburg Vintage bowls, this Northwood pattern does have several distinctive qualities of its own. The most obvious one is of course the grape-leaf center with grapes around its edge. Also missing are the usual tendrils and the small leaflets and the exterior doesn't carry a hobnail pattern but a typical near cut design.

Heart and Trees

Heart and Vine

Heart and Flowers

Heavy Banded Diamonds

Heavy Diamond

Heavy Grape

HEAVY HOBNAIL

I first showed this unusual item in my rarities book. At that time, only the white version was known but since then a spectacular purple example has been seen. These were the Fenton Rustic vases that weren't pulled or slung into the vase shape and very few are known.

HEAVY IRIS

I'm sure every collector of carnival glass has speculated at one time or another over the maker of this beautiful pattern. Some have felt Millersburg, others Fenton. Now, however, it is with some assurance we report that a very sizeable chunk of a Heavy Iris tumbler was unearthed at the Dugan dump site in 1975 so we can declare it a Dugan pattern. The only shape is, of course, a graceful tankard water set. The design is sharp and heavy, simple enough to be effective yet covering much of the available space. The colors are marigold, purple and white with purple the most desired. All in all, a beautiful set to own.

HEAVY PINEAPPLE

I feel very happy to show this Fenton rarity because it is only the second example in carnival glass to be reported. This one is a beautiful frosty white while the other was cobalt blue. Both pieces are large 10" bowls on three feet. The design is all exterior and heavily raised. Certainly there must be other examples of Heavy Pineapple but if so, they haven't been reported.

HEAVY PRISMS

This beautiful celery vase stands 6" tall and shows the quality English carnival glass makers attained. The maker is Davisons and the colors reported are marigold, amethyst, and blue. The glass is very thick and heavy and the luster top notch.

HEAVY SHELL

Found only on White Carnival, this Dugan pattern is rather scarce. The shapes are oval bowls and matching candlesticks. The glass is quite heavy and the luster very rich.

HEAVY WEB

Found primarily on large, thick bowls in peach opalescent, Heavy Web is a very interesting Dugan pattern. It has been found with two distinct exterior patterns — a beautifully realistic grape and leaf design covering most of the surface and an equally attractive morning glory pattern. I've seen various shapes including round, ruffled, square and elongated ones. A vivid purple or green bowl in this pattern would certainly be a treasure.

Heavy Hobnail

Heavy Iris

Heavy Pineapple

Heavy Prisms

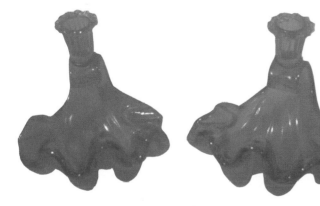

Heavy Shell

Heavy Web

HERON

Like the Fisherman Mug shown elsewhere in this book, the Dugan attribution is sheer speculation and has been arrived at only by the process of elimination. They simply do not look like products of any of the other known companies that made sizeable amounts of iridized glass. Known only in amethyst, and a very rare marigold, these mugs are much harder to find and must be considered rare. The pattern is on one side of the mug only.

HOBNAIL

While plentiful in many other types of glass, Hobnail is quite a rare item in carnival and one of real beauty. The very pattern seems perfectly suited for iridescence. The base carries a many rayed design and all the pieces I've seen are top-notch. The pitchers and tumblers are very rare and extremely hard to locate but even the rose bowl is a prize and the Lady's spittoon is a little darling. Hobnail was made by Millersburg.

> Shapes: Water sets
> Rosebowls
> Ladies spittoons
> Vases
> Table sets

HOBNAIL SODA GOLD

While most spittoons found in Carnival Glass are of a daintier size, Imperial's Hobnail Soda Gold spittoon is a larger, more practical size. It measures 7″ across the top and stands 5″ high. I've seen examples in marigold and green as well as a peculiar dark shade of amber. Many of these have a great deal of wear on the bottom indicating they were actually used!

HOBSTAR

Apparently this was one of the early near-cut patterns from Imperial. I'd guess it experienced great popularity from the first for it was carried over from crystal to Carnival Glass in many shapes, including berry sets, cookie jars, table sets, bride's baskets and a very rare pickle caster in an ornate holder. Marigold is the common color with purple and green quite scarce.

HOBSTAR AND ARCHES

Here is another well-done geometric design from the Imperial Company. Found mostly in bowls, a two piece fruit bowl is available, as shown. Please note the base is the same as that of the Long Hobstar set. Both are correct and it wasn't unusual for a company to get double mileage where possible. Colors are marigold, green, amethyst, and smoke.

HOBSTAR AND CUT TRIANGLES

This very unusual pattern is typically English in design, with strong contrast between geometrically patterned areas against very plain areas. Rose Presznick lists bowls, plates, and a rosebowl in this pattern in both green and amethyst but the only shapes I've seen are bowls, rosebowls, and compotes in marigold or amethyst.

Heron

Hobnail

Hobnail Soda Gold

Hobstar

Hobstar and Arches

Hobstar and Cut Triangles

HOBSTAR AND FEATHER

If one word could be summoned to describe this Millersburg pattern, that word would be "massive." The glass is thick, the near-cut design deeply cut and impressive. Whether it is a punch bowl, a giant rosebowl or a pulled vase whimsey, the Hobstar and Feather pattern is not likely to be confused with any other. The usual colors of marigold, green and amethyst are to be found and always in a fine radium finish.

> Other shapes: Covered Butter
> Sugar
> Creamer
> Spooner
> 5" Bowl — Round
> Heart Shaped 5" Bowl
> Compote
> Large Bowl

HOBSTAR AND FRUIT

This Dugan pattern is known on small and large bowls and a rare 10½" plate. The bowls are found in peach opalescent mostly, but the small bowl is known in aqua opalescent and the plate has been found in ice blue.

HOBSTAR BAND

This scarce Imperial pattern is found only on handled celery vases and water sets of two varieties. The usual pitcher is flat based, but as you can see a quite rare pedestal footed variant is known. The only color reported is a good rich marigold.

HOBSTAR FLOWER

This beautiful little Northwood compote is seldom seen and usually comes as a surprise to most collectors. I've heard it called "Octagon" or "Fashion" at one time or another, and most people say they've never seen it before. It is a rather hard to find item. It is shown in marigold but is mostly found in amethyst.

HOBSTAR PANELS

Apparently the English glassmakers like the creamer shape, for they certainly made their share of them. Here is a well-conceived geometric design with hobstars, sunbursts, and panels integrated into a very nice whole. The only color I've seen is the deep marigold shown, but certainly there may be others.

HOBSTAR REVERSED

Shown is what was called a "sideboard set" in the advertising by Davisons of Gateshead. It consists of a flower frog and holder that is footed and two side vases which were also used as spooners. Also known is a covered butterdish. The colors listed are marigold, amethyst, and blue, but not all colors are found in all shapes.

Hobstar and Feather

Hobstar and Fruit

Hobstar Band

Hobstar Flower

Hobstar Panels

Hobstar Reversed

INTERIOR RAYS

While I can't be sure this is Australian, this set comes from there. Shown is a covered butter, covered sugar, and covered jam jar but other shapes may exist.

INVERTED COIN DOT

The tumbler shown is part of a scarce water set made by the Fenton company and to the best of my knowledge is not found in other shapes. As you can see, the pattern is all interior. Colors known are marigold, amethyst and green but blue may exist.

INVERTED FEATHER

This is probably the best known of all Cambridge carnival glass patterns and is found in a variety of shapes including a cracker jar, table set, water set, compote, sherbet, wine, milk pitcher, and punch set. All shapes are rare except the cracker jar and colors known are marigold, green, and amethyst.

INVERTED STRAWBERRY

Like its cousin, Inverted Thistle, this beautiful Cambridge pattern is all intaglio and can be found on several shapes including berry sets, water sets, candlesticks, large compotes, sherbets, milk pitchers, creamers, spooners, a stemmed celery, powder jars, and a ladies spittoon. All shapes are rare and colors known are marigold, green, amethyst, and blue.

INVERTED THISTLE

Cambridge was responsible for very original patterns and superior workmanship and here is a prime example. Known in water sets, a spittoon, a covered box, a pickle dish, and a breakfast set, this is an intaglio pattern. Colors are marigold, amethyst, green, and a rare blue.

IRIS

Along with the plain Buttermilk Goblet, this pattern found in both compotes and goblets, has created a good deal of controversy, for some have felt it was a Millersburg product. However, I'm convinced it is Fenton. Colors seen are marigold, green, amethyst, and the very rare white example shown.

Interior Rays

Inverted Coin Dot

Inverted Feather

Inverted Strawberry

Inverted Thistle (Late)

Iris

ISAAC BENESCH BOWL

This cute 6¼″ advertising bowl is quite easily identified because of its distinct design. It bears the labeling "The Great House of Isaac Benesch and Sons, Wilksbarre, Pa., Baltimore, Md., Annapolis, Md." The center theme is bracketed by sprigs of daisy-like blossoms and leaves. The exterior carries the familiar wide panel design and a rayed base. The predominant color is amethyst. This was made by Millersburg.

JACK-IN-THE-PULPIT

While both Dugan and Fenton made Jack-in-the-Pulpit vases, the one shown is a Northwood pattern and is so marked. It stands 8¼″ tall and has an exterior ribbing. Colors known are marigold, purple, green, aqua opalestent, and white but others may exist.

JACKMAN WHISKEY

Much like its cousin, the Golden Wedding bottle, this was designed to hold whiskey for commercial sale. It is scarcer than the former and generally has better iridescence. The maker is unknown.

JELLY JAR

For years I found the lids to these Imperial Jelly Jars in shops and thought they were late carnival glass "coasters", but a few years back, I saw the two parts put together and was really quite surprised at what I saw. The jar itself is 3″ wide and 2¾″ tall and of deep, well iridized marigold. All the pattern is interior so that when the jar was upended onto the lid, a design was formed in the jelly. The lid itself also carries an interior design of spokes and an exterior one of a many-rayed star. Again, here is a true rarity, well within any collector's range.

JEWELED HEART

Carried over from the pressed glass era, Jeweled Heart is, of course, the famous exterior pattern of the Farmyard bowl. However, Dugan used it as a primary pattern on very scarce water sets when the pitcher is footed — an uncommon shape for water pitchers in Carnival glass. I have seen Jeweled Heart in purple, peach, and marigold but other colors may exist. If so, they would be considered ultra-rare. A tumbler is reported in white but I haven't seen it.

JEWELS

While there are many shapes in the Imperial Jewels line of glass, I do not really consider them Carnival Glass any more than I consider stretch glass as Carnival. However, I will show one example, a beautiful butterscotch fan vase, to illustrate the effectiveness of this beautifully iridized art glass.

Isaac Benesch Bowl

Jack-In-the-Pulpit

Jackman Whiskey

Jelly Jar

Jeweled Heart

Jewels

KIWI

This very
mountain-ra
marigold.

KNOTTED

In many w
tern for the
marigold, blu

KOOKABU

Similar to
wattle, and t

KOOKABU

In this Aus
circle. And of

L B J HAT

This late C
3″ tall. While

LACY DEV

Reported
Carnival sh
bowls.

MALAGA

Malaga is a rather difficult pattern to find, indicating production must have been small on this Dugan design. What a pity for the all-over grape pattern is a good one with imaginative detail throughout. Found only on large bowls and plates, I've heard of colors of marigold, amber and purple only, but green is a strong possibility.

MALLARD DUCK

I certainly wish I knew more about this rare item but it's the only true Carnival one I've seen. I believe these were made by Tiffin (mostly in milk glass) and I once saw an example with applied ruby lustre. However, I can say with assurance the one shown is old, has been in one of the country's major collections for years and is a prized rarity of the owner. The coloring is a beautiful clambroth with fiery blue and pink highlights.

MANY FRUITS

This is a truly lovely fruit pattern, something that any company would be proud to claim. The mold work is heavy and distinct, the design is interesting and quite realistic and the coloration flawless. I personally prefer the ruffled base, but that is a small matter. This Dugan pattern would have made a beautiful water set. The colors are marigold, blue, white, purple and green.

MANY STARS

Which came first — the chicken or the egg? Or in this case, the Many Stars or the Bernheimer bowl? For they are exactly the same except for the center design where in the former a large star replaces the advertising. These bowls are generous in size and can be found in amethyst, green, marigold and blue. The green is often a light, airy shade just a bit darker than an ice green and is very attractive when found with a gold iridescence. Millersburg manufactured this pattern.

MAPLE LEAF

Maple Leaf is a carry-over pattern from the custard glass line, but in carnival glass is limited to stemmed berry sets, table sets and water sets. I examined shards of this pattern from the Dugan dump site, so items in carnival glass were obviously turned out at that factory, probably for the Northwood Company. At any rate, the background is the same Soda Gold pattern as that found on the exterior of Garden Path bowls and plates. Maple Leaf was made in marigold, purple, cobalt blue and green.

MARILYN

This water set pattern is probably one of the most unusual and outstanding in the field of carnival glass. First look at the pitcher's shape. Notice the unusual upper edging, so different than those of other companies. Then there is the drooping pouring lip so favored by the Millersburg company. The finish is, of course, the fine radium look and the glass is heavy. All in all, a real prize for any collector.

Malaga

Mallard Duck

Many Fruits

Many Stars

Maple Leaf

Marilyn

CAMBRIDGE #2351

Shown is a single punch cup of this rare Cambridge pattern. The set was made in marigold, amethyst, and green. The quantities produced were quite small, so few pieces exist today.

OCTAGON

Next to the Fashion pattern, this is probably Imperial's most common near-cut design, especially when found in marigold. But dark colors now and then show up and the shape shown, the toothpick, is rare in marigold. In the beautiful purple, the toothpick is extremely rare. Octagon is found in table sets, water sets, wine sets, footed vases, milk pitchers, goblets, and the rare toothpicks. It is a pleasing all-over pattern.

OCTET

Even if this pattern were not marked, we would attribute it to the Northwood Company because the exterior pattern is the Northwood vintage found on the Star of David and Bows bowl. Octet is also a dome-footed bowl, usually about 8½″ in diameter. It is a simple, but effective pattern — one that wouldn't be easily confused with others. The colors are marigold, purple, green, white, and ice green. The purple is most common.

OHIO STAR

This beauitful near-cut vase is almost ten inches tall and certainly is a stand-out in the carnival vase field. While the majority of vases are of simple design, this one flaunts its multi-cut pattern even to the star in the high domed base. The coloring is excellent and not only is Ohio Star found in the usual marigold, green, purple and rare blue but as reported in a beautiful frosty white! Certainly Millersburg pastels are not easily found and one of these would enhance any collection.

OLYMPIC COMPOTE

The Millersburg Olympic miniature compote is **extremely** rare and to date I've been privileged to see only this one. Its measurements are the same as the Leaf and Little Flowers compote made by the same company and the exterior and base are identical also. If ever the old adage "Great things come in small packages" could apply, certainly it would be to the Olympic compote.

OPEN EDGE BASKET

This rather common Fenton pattern is found quite frequently in several sizes and colors, especially blue, marigold, green, and amethyst. But pink, ice blue, ice green, white and red examples do exist in variously shaped items including hat shapes, vase whimseys, banana boat whimseys and bowl shapes. The interior may be plain or carry the Blackberry pattern and sometimes advertising is present.

Cambridge #2351

Octagon

Octet

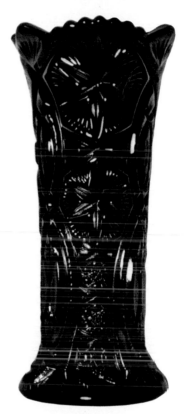

Ohio Star

Olympic Compote

Open Edge Basket

OPEN ROSE

This pattern is very similar to the Lustre Rose pattern but is not found on the wide range of shapes as the latter. The plate shown is the most sought shape but there are also footed and flat bowls of many sizes available. Colors of marigold, smoke, green, purple, clambroth, and amber are known and each is usually outstanding. The amber plate shown typifies the Imperial quality.

OPTIC AND BUTTONS

In crystal, this pattern is found in many shapes, including table sets, plates, oil bottles, decanters, shakers and sherbets, but in Carnival Glass Optic and Buttons is limited to berry sets, a goblet, large handled bowl, a small pitcher, tumblers in two shapes and a rare cup and saucer. Many of the items in carnival are marked with the Imperial "iron cross" mark, including the milk pitcher and the cup. All shapes I've seen are in marigold only.

OPTIC FLUTE

This Imperial pattern is seldom mentioned, but can be found on berry sets as shown. Colors I've seen are marigold and smoke but others may have been made.

ORANGE PEEL

While many people feel this is a Fenton pattern, I'm inclined to believe both Orange Peel and Fruit Salad are products of the Dugan Company. Orange Peel is found in punch sets, custard sets, and stemmed desserts in both a rich marigold and green.

ORANGE TREE

No other Fenton pattern had more popularity or was made in more shapes than the Orange Tree and all its variants. Known in berry sets, table sets, water sets, ice cream sets, breakfast sets, compotes, mugs, plates, powder jars, hatpin holders, rose bowls, a loving cup, wines, punch sets and goblets, Orange Tree is found in marigold, blue, green, amethyst, peach opalescent, milk glass lustered, aqua opalescent, white, amber, vaseline, aqua, red, and amberina.

ORANGE TREE AND SCROLL

What a beauty this hard to find tankard water set is. The Orange Trees are like those on the regular pieces and the Orange Tree Orchard set, but below the trees are panels of scroll work much like the design on the Milady pattern. Colors are marigold, blue, and green but I wouldn't rule out amethyst or white on this Fenton product.

Open Rose

Optic and Buttons

Optic Flute

Orange Peel

Orange Tree

Orange Tree and Scroll

POINSETTIA

Found only on one shape (the beautiful milk pitcher shown), Poinsettia is an outstanding Imperial pattern. Standing 6½" tall, the Poinsettia is usually found in marigold or smoke color, but as you can see, a rare and beautiful purple does exist as does an equally rare green. What a shame more shapes do not exist in this beautiful design!

POINSETTIA

For some reason, in years past, someone attributed this very stylish pattern to the Fenton Glass Company. Just why, I can't guess for Poinsettia was made by Northwood in custard glass and was illustrated in their advertising of the day. At any rate, this mistake has been corrected and we now recognize this well-done bowl as a Harry Northwood design. Poinsettia if found either as a flat based or footed bowl with the Fine Rib as an exterior pattern. The finish is nearly always superior. The colors are marigold, green, purple, fiery amethyst, white and ice green.

POINSETTIA, INTERIOR

Here is something unusual — a tumbler with all the pattern on the inside. Of course, we've all seen the Northwood Swirl pattern which is also an interior one, but that was a simple geometrical design while the Interior Poinsettia is an offering of a large flower. Apparently these were never very popular for they are very scarce. Also, to the best of my knowledge, no pitcher has been found. The iridescence is on both the inside and outside and is a good rich marigold. Only some of these Northwood tumblers are marked.

POND LILY

Much like other Fenton patterns such as Two Flowers and Water Lily, Pond Lily has both scale filler and the Lotus-like flower. The only shape I've seen is the bon-bon and colors reported are marigold, blue, green, and white. Of course other colors may exist and certainly red is a possibility.

PONY

For years the origin of this attractive bowl has been questioned and only recently has it been attributed to the Dugan Company. Colors seen are marigold, amethyst, and ice green. The mold work is quite good.

POPPY

Large open compotes seem to have a fascination all their own and this one from Millersburg is certainly no exception. It is quality all the way whether found in green, purple, or marigold. Standing 7" tall and being 8" across, Poppy has four mold marks. It often has the Potpurri as a secondary pattern. The poppy flowers and leaves are well done and are stippled.

Poinsettia

Poinsettia

Poinsettia, Interior

Pond Lily

Pony

Poppy

POPPY

This Northwood pattern is most often found on small oval bowls, described as trays or, with the sides crimped, as pickle dishes. However, it is also found as an exterior pattern on larger bowls, some with plain interiors, others with a large Daisy in the center of the bowl. The colors are electric blue, marigold, peach, purple, and white. Others may exist but these are the ones I've seen.

POPPY SHOW

Let me state from the beginning this is not the same pattern as the Poppy Show Vase. It is a beautiful, well-made item, very much akin to the Rose Show pattern in concept and design. It is found only on large bowls and plates in a wide range of colors, including marigold, green, blue, purple, white, ice blue, and ice green. This Northwood pattern brings top dollar whenever offered for sale.

POPPY SHOW VASE

What a shame this beauty was chosen to be reproduced by Imperial in the 60s! The old Poppy Show Vase is a real show stopper, standing about 12″ tall, with a lip diameter of 6¾″! The mold work is very fine, with the graceful poppy in a series of four panels around the vase. I've seen this artistic gem in marigold, clambroth, pastel marigold, amber, green, and purple. Naturally, the darker colors are quite scarce and are priced accordingly.

PRAYER RUG

Known only in the finish shown, beautiful custard glass with a marigold iridescence, Fenton's Prayer Rug is a seldom seen item. The only shape is a handled bon-bon, but I suspect time will bring to light additional ones since uniridized pieces are known in small bowls, vases and hat shapes.

PREMIUM

Not only found in the well-known candlesticks shown, but also in 8½″ bowls, 12″ bowls and 14″ plates. Imperial's Premium pattern is shown in old catalogs in marigold, clambroth, purple, green, and smoke. The candlesticks are 8½″ tall, heavy, and beautifully iridized! While not in the class with the Grape and Cable candlesticks, they are still quite nice. Used with the medium size bowl, they make a nice console set.

PRETTY PANELS

This is a marked Northwood tumbler and as such is quite a sight for tumbler collectors. The color is a very bold frosty green and the enameled cherry design is above average. It is found in marigold also.

Poppy

Poppy Show

Poppy Show Vase

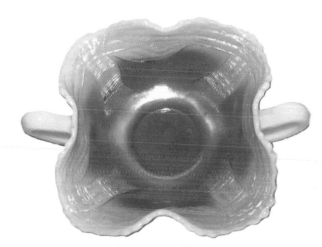

Prayer Rug

Premium

Pretty Panels

PRIMROSE

For some reason, this Millersburg pattern hasn't received the "raves" it might and I can't understand why. I have one and treasure it just as much as I do a Nesting Swan. The glass work is equally as good and the iridescence excellent. The reverse pattern is Fine Cut Hearts and the two blend beautifully. Primrose is found primarily on large bowls in the three main Millersburg colors, plus the spectacular blue shown.

PRIMROSE AND FISHNET (#2475)

This unusual Imperial pattern has two kissing cousins, also in red carnival; one showing grapes, the other roses. The floral design is on one side only and the fishnet covers the remainder of the glass. While red is the only reported color in iridized glass, all three patterns are known in crystal. The Primrose and Fishnet vase stands 6″ tall. Needless to say, they are quite scarce.

PRISM AND CANE

This very scarce product of Sowerbys has an interior pattern of Embossed Scroll variant and, as you can see, the base is ground. Apparently it is a sauce dish or jam dish as it measures 5″ across the rim and stands 2¼″ tall.

PRISM AND DAISY BAND

Apparently one of Imperial's late designs in carnival glass and intended for a cheap mass sale, Prism and Daisy Band can be found only in marigold in berry sets, breakfast sets, a stemmed compote and a vase shape. The coloring is adequate but not superior.

PRISMS

We now have evidence to support a Northwood origin for this unusual little compote. For quite awhile amethyst was the only color seen, but here is a marigold of which I've seen some four or five, and green also exists. Prisms measure 7¼″ across the handles and is 2½″ tall. The pattern is all exterior and is intaglio with an ornate star under the base like the one on the Cherry and Cable butter dish.

PROPELLER

Besides the usual small compote found in this Imperial pattern, I'm very happy to show the rare 7½″ stemmed vase in the Propeller pattern. The coloring is a good rich marigold, but others may exist since the compote is seen in marigold, green, and amethyst.

Primrose

Primrose and Fishnet

Prism and Cane

Prism and Daisy Band

Prisms

Propeller

PULLED HUSK CORN VASE

Apparently Harry Northwood wasn't quite satisfied with this very rare example of a corn vase, for few of these are around in comparison with the regular corn vase. Known in two sizes, the Pulled Husk vase has been seen in green and purple and some are pulled more grotesquely than others.

PULLED LOOP

This rather simple Fenton vase design is found quite often, mostly in marigold, blue, or amethyst, but it is known in a beautiful green, as well as an occasional peach opalescent finish. The size may vary from 8" to 12", but the finish is usually very heavily lustered.

PUZZLE

Found in stemmed bon-bons and compotes, Dugan's Puzzle is an appealing pattern. The all-over design is well balanced and the stippling adds interest. Colors known are marigold, purple, green, blue, white, and peach opalescent.

QUESTION MARKS

Here is a simple Dugan pattern found on the interiors of bon bons and occasionally compotes like the one shown. Again the exterior is usually plain and the colors are peach opalescent, marigold, purple, and white. Both the compote and the bon bon are footed; the compote is one of the small size, measuring 4½" tall and 4" across the highly ruffled edge. The exterior occasionally has a pattern called Georgia Belle.

QUILL

Once again we show a pattern of which shards were found in the Dugan diggings and I truly believe Quill was indeed a Dugan Glass Company pattern. The pitcher is some 10" tall and has a base diameter of 4½". The colors are marigold and amethyst and the iridescence is usually above average. Quill is a scarce pattern and apparently small quantities were made, again pointing toward the Dugan Company as the manufacturer. The water set is the only shape.

RAGGED ROBIN

Just why more of these Fenton bowls weren't produced is a mystery, but the fact remains these are quite hard to find today. Found only on average size bowls often with a ribbon candy edge. Colors reported are marigold, blue, green, and white with blue most available.

Pulled Husk Corn Vase

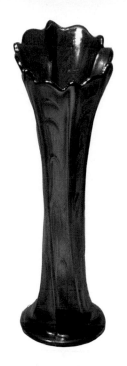

Pulled Loop

Puzzle

Question Marks

Quill

Ragged Robin

RAINDROPS

Here is another of the dome footed bowls Dugan available in peach opalescent like so many offered by the Dugan Company. Remember, I said earlier that I felt Dugan was responsible for at least 90% of the peach carnival and a close study of these bowls will support this belief. Raindrops is found without stippling. It has the Keyhole pattern as an exterior companion and has four mold marks. All in all, it is a nice pattern to own, especially if you like peach opalescent glass.

RAMBLER ROSE

Until quite recently, I'd always felt Rambler Rose was a Fenton product, but upon examining a large shard of this pattern from the Dugan dump site, I'm compelled to admit my mistake. This water set has a bulbous pitcher with a ruffled top. The flowers are well designed and clearly molded. The colors are marigold, purple, blue, and green. Perhaps research in the years ahead will add more information about this pattern.

RANGER

Ranger is another of those strange Imperial patterns shown in their old catalogs, and bearing the M inside a C mark like the Oklahoma tumbler and the Voltive Light vase. As you can see, the color is good and the only shapes I'm familiar with are a tumbler, pitcher, syrup, creamer and sugar, although the old catalogs list vases, compotes, berry sets, water sets and a cracker jar in crystal.

RASPBERRY

Even without the famous trademark, this pattern would be recognized as a Northwood product, for it includes the basket-weave so often found on that company's designs. Available in water sets, table sets, berry sets, and a milk pitcher, Raspberry has long been a favorite with collectors. The colors are marigold, green, purple, ice blue, and ice green with the richly lustered Purple most prevalent.

RAYS AND RIBBON

Each of the makers of carnival glass seems to have had a try at a pattern using stippled rays. The Millersburg version is quite distinctive because of the bordering of ribbon-like design, resembling a fleur-de-lis design. Most of these bowls are not radium finish and usually carry the Cactus pattern on the exterior. Occasionally a plate is found in Rays and Ribbons, but one wonders if this were not produced as a shallow bowl. Amethyst is the usual color, followed by green, marigold, and vaseline in that order.

SHAPES: Bowls
Plates

RIBBON TIE

Sometimes called Comet, this well-known Fenton pattern is found chiefly on all sorts of bowls as well as ruffled plates. The colors range from very good to poor in marigold, blue, amethyst, red, and green and often the luster is only so-so.

Raindrops

Rambler Rose

Ranger

Raspberry

Rays and Ribbons

Ribbon Tie

RIPPLE

This Imperial pattern is fairly common in marigold, clear or amethyst glass but the teal color shown is a real exception and quite a beauty. Ranging in height from 10″ to 16″, the Ripple vase depends on what design it has, in the "pulling" or "slinging" of the glass while hot and, naturally, the taller the vase, the less design exists.

RISING SUN

This very unusual pattern has been seen in both the marigold shown and cobalt blue. The pitcher is found in two variations, one with a pedestal base, the other as shown. A matching tray has been reported but I haven't seen it. The maker has not been confirmed at this time.

ROBIN

Despite the reproductions of this fine old Imperial pattern, the prices have held up rather well on the old pieces. The water sets, found only in marigold, and the mug found in smoke are especially desirable. Apparently the appeal lies in the handsome presentation of the nicely done bird, the flower and branch dividers, and the flowering leaf pattern, so pleasing to the eye.

ROCOCO

This beautiful little Imperial vase was the first item in smoke I'd ever seen and I must admit I loved it at first sight! While it may be found on a small bowl shape with a dome base, and in marigold as well as smoke, it is the vase most of us think of whenever Rococo is mentioned. The vase is 5½″ tall and shows four mold marks. I have had a green one reported but haven't seen it yet.

ROMAN ROSETTE GOBLET (UNLISTED)

While this pattern is not difficult to find in pressed glass, this is the only reported item in iridized glass to the best of my knowledge. As you can see, it is slightly crooked but the iridization on the clear glass is unmistakable with beautiful blue and pink coloring. It measures 6″ tall and has a base diameter of 2¾″.

ROSALIND

Many people know this pattern as Drape and Tie and I first believed it to be an Imperial pattern but it is definitely Millersburg and is found on large bowls as well as the interior pattern of the Dolphins compote. When found on large shallow bowls, it usually carries a wide panel exterior and a many-rayed star base.

Other Shapes: Jelly Compote 5″
Compote 8″

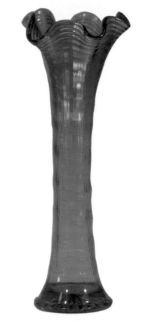

Ripple

Rising Sun

Robin

Rococo

Roman Rosette Goblet

Rosalind

ROSE AND GREEK KEY PLATE

This very beautiful square plate is a sight to behold. Not only is it quite unique but so very well designed that I simply can not understand why there aren't more of these. But alas, there's only the one known. The coloring is a smoky amber. The plate measures 8½" across and the roses are deep and hollow on the underside, much like the well-known Rose Show bowls.

ROSE COLUMN

This stately Millersburg vase is a real beauty and like several carnival patterns such as the Imperial Grape Carafe or the Grape Arbor pitcher, the rows of roses are hollow. This required great skill by the worker when removing it from the mold and many must have been broken in doing so. This lovely vase is 10" tall and 5" across the diameter. There are six columns of roses, each topped by a sprig of leaves. The iridescence is top-quality and the colors are marigold, blue, green, and amethyst. The Rose Column vase would make a lovely companion to the People's Vase.

ROSE GARDEN

I'm sure most collectors have heard of the pitcher in this English pattern and there is a collection plateau and vase too. I've had a covered butter dish reported but haven't personally seen it. Here is the rare 6" deep bowl that hasn't been listed until now. The pattern is intaglio and the colors are marigold or cobalt blue. Rose Garden always brings a premium price when sold.

ROSE SHOW

What a handsome piece of glass this is! The design of this Northwood is flawless, heavy, and covering every inch of available space. Yet it isn't in the least bit busy-looking. One has the distinct feeling he is looking into a reeded basket of fresh-cut roses and can almost smell the perfume. Found only on bowls and a plate variant, the beautiful pattern was produced in small amounts in marigold, purple, blue, green, white, ice blue, ice green, peach opalescent, amber, aqua opalescent, and a rare ice green opalescent.

ROSE SPRAY COMPOTE

Standing only 4½" at its tallest point, this beautiful compote is a real treasure. The only colors I've heard about are the beautiful ice blue and ice green. I suspect this is a Fenton product, but have no verification of this. The rose and leaf spray is on one side of the rim only and is rather faint, much like the Kittens bowls.

ROSE TREE

Make no mistake about it, this is a very scarce and desirable Fenton bowl pattern. I believe this was the Fenton answer to the Imperial Lustre Rose, but apparently it was made in small quantities. The colors known are marigold and cobalt blue and the size is a generous 10" diameter.

Rose and Greek Key Plate

Rose Column

Rose Garden

Rose Show

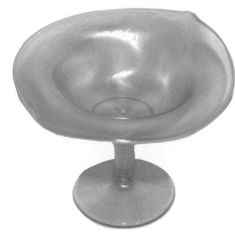

Rose Spray Compote

Rose Tree

ROSES AND FRUIT

This beautiful little compote is unique in several ways and is a very hard to find Millersburg item. It measures 5¼″ from handle to handle and is nearly 4″ high. Notice the deep bowl effect (so often used by Millersburg on compote and bon-bons) and the pedestal base. In addition, observe the unusual stippling around the edge of the interior and of course the combination of roses, berries, and pears are quite distinltive. It is found in green and amethyst mostly, but was made in marigold as well.

ROSES AND RUFFLES LAMP (RED)

I'm frankly not too taken with Gone With the Wind Lamps, but the beautifully iridized ones are in a class by themselves and the very few red ones known are simply beautiful. The Roses and Ruffles lamp is 22″ tall. It has excellent fittings of brass and is quality all the way. The mold work on the glass is quite beautiful and the lustre superior.

ROSETTE

Combining several well-known carnival glass patterns, including Stippled Rays, Beads, and Prisms, this Northwood pattern isn't the easiest thing to find. In arrangement, it reminds one of the Greek Key pattern, but Rosette stands on its own. Found only on generous sized bowls, the colors are marigold and amethyst. Green may be a possibility, but I haven't seen one.

ROUND-UP

As I stated earlier, Round-up, Fanciful and Apple Blossom Twigs all have the same exterior pattern and shards of the latter two were found in the Dugan diggings. Found only on bowls, ruffled plates and true plates, Round-up is available in marigold, purple, peach opalescent, blue, amber, white and a pale shade of lavender. The true plate is quite scarce and always brings top dollar.

ROYALTY

Perhaps one might mistake this for the Fashion pattern at first glance but with a little concentrated study, it becomes obvious they aren't the same. Royalty is a pattern formed from a series of hobstars above a series of diamond panels. Found on punch sets and two piece fruit bowls, this Imperial pattern is mostly found in marigold, but the fruit bowl set has been reported in smoke.

RUFFLED RIB SPITTOON

This little Northwood cutie could be called Fine Rib or Lustre and Clear I guess but I feel the name given is more appropriate. At any rate the coloring is a good rich marigold and the ribbing is on the interior. The spittoon stands 4″ tall and has a rim diameter of 4½″ with a collar base diameter of nearly 2″.

Rose and Fruit

Roses and Ruffles Lamp

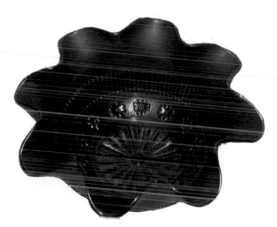

Rosette

Round-up

Royalty

Ruffled Rib Spittoon

RUSTIC

I would venture to say Rustic is one of the best known and most common of vase shapes for it is plentiful, found in many sizes and colors including marigold, blue, green, amethyst, aqua, vaseline, amber, white, peach opalescent, and red. It was pulled from the Fenton Hobnail vase shapes and can be found in sizes from 6″ to 20″.

S-REPEAT

Made in crystal, decorated crystal, and gilt glass prior to being made in Carnival Glass, S-Repeat is found in only a small range of shapes in iridized glass. Besides the punch set shown, there is a rare toothpick that has been widely reproduced and a handful of marigold tumblers that some believe are questionable. At any rate, in carnival glass, Dugan's S-Repeat is a very scarce item.

SACIC ASHTRAY

This little ash tray is a real mystery in many ways. It reads: "NARAJA SACIC POMELO" Apparently it was meant to go to Brazil, but why an English glass maker would mold such an item escapes me. The color is quite good, with a touch of amber in the marigold.

SAILBOATS

Found in small bowls, plates, compotes, goblets, and wines, Sailboats is a well-known Fenton pattern that competes nicely with Imperial's Windmill pattern. Colors I've heard about are marigold, blue, green, vaseline, amber and red, but not all colors are found in all shapes.

SCALE BAND

While not too original, this Fenton pattern of smooth rays and bands of scale filler does quite nicely in the shapes chosen; bowls, plates, pitchers and tumblers. The color most seen is, of course, marigold; however, Scale Band can also be found in green, amethyst, peach opalescent, aqua opalescent (quite rare) and red.

SCALES

Most of these Northwood bowls I've seen are small — 6″ to 7″ in diameter. Nevertheless, they are well done, interesting items and add much to any collection. The Fishscale pattern is on the interior while the Beads design is on the exterior. When held to the light, one pattern fits happily into position to compliment the whole, giving a pleasant experience.

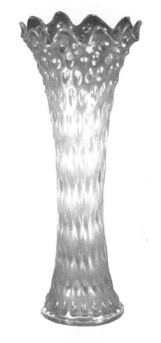

Rustic

S-Repeat

Sacic Ashtray

Sailboats

Scale Band

Scales

SCOTCH THISTLE

What a pretty pattern this is for the interior of a compote! As you can see, the exterior is plain like so many compotes but the edges have a very interesting ruffles effect. Colors I've seen are marigold, blue, green, and amethyst but others may certainly exist. This pattern was manufactured by Fenton.

SCROLL AND FLOWER PANELS

I've always been intrigued by this stylish Imperial pattern even though it was reproduced in the 60s with a flared top. As you can see, the mold work, while very busy, is quite satisfying and the coloring is super. I've seen this vase in marigold and purple, but green is a possibility. The vase stands 10″ tall on a collar base with a many-rayed star.

SCROLL EMBOSSED

As I said earlier, while this pattern originated at the Imperial factory, it was later produced in England on carnival glass, notably on the Diving Dolphins bowl and on a four-handled sauce dish. The Imperial Version is used with File pattern exterior on bowls, with Eastern Star as an exterior pattern on large compotes, as well as alone on bowls and smaller compotes. The usual colors are green, marigold, or purple, but smoke does exist. A scarce plate shape is shown.

SCROLL EMBOSSED VT.

Much like its Imperial counterpart this English version is found on small bowls, small handled ashtrays, compotes, and the Diving Dolphins bowls. Without the exterior design, it would be impossible to say who made which, however the English version is known in marigold, blue, green, and amethyst.

SEA GULLS BOWL

If one rarity in this book stands as an example of "scarce but not prized", the Sea Gulls bowl is that rarity. Certainly there are far less of these to be found than many items that bring 10 times the money, but for some strange reason, these cuties are not sought by most collectors. The two bird figures are heavily detailed as is the bowl pattern. The color, while not outstanding, is good and is iridized both inside and out. The diameter of the bowl is 5¾″ and the depth is 2⅞″. I believe the manufacturer was Jeanette but I could be wrong.

SEA GULLS VASE

Here is another seldom found English vase pattern, quite original and closely approaching the art glass field. The only color reported is a good marigold.

Scotch Thistle

Scroll and Flower Panels

Scroll Embossed

Scroll Embossed Vt.

Sea Gulls Bowl

Sea Gulls Vase

SEACOAST PINTRAY

Pintrays are not common in carnival glass and this one from Millersburg is one of the nicest ones. The irregular shaping, the beautiful coloring and fine detail make this an outstanding item. It measures 5½" by 3¾" and rests on an oval collar base. The colors are marigold, green, amethyst and a fine deep purple.

SEAWEED

Can you imagine a more graceful pattern than this one from Millersburg? The curving leaves and snail-like figures seem to be drifting back and forth in the watery depths and the bubbles of beading add just the right touch. Usually found on fairly large bowls, Seaweed has three mold marks. The colors are marigold, green and amethyst. Also a rare plate, and a rarer small bowl have been found.

SEAWEED LAMP

I've heard of four of these lamps in two different base shapes, but all with the Seaweed design circling the body. All were in marigold ranging from quite good to poor. The example shown measures 12" to the top of the font. The maker is unknown but the lamp is a rare one.

SHELL

I've always felt this was a superior Imperial pattern — simple yet effective. This is especially true on the few plates I've seen. The pattern is a well-balanced one of eight scalloped shells around a star-like pattern. The background may or may not be stippled — I've seen it both ways. The shapes are smallish bowls, plates, and a reported compote I haven't seen. The colors are marigold, green, purple, smoke, and amber.

SHELL AND JEWEL

Easily found, this Westmoreland pattern was made only in the shapes shown in colors of marigold, amethyst, and green (white has been reported but not confirmed). The pattern is a copy of the Nugget Ware pattern of the Dominion Glass Company of Canada. Shell and Jewel has been reproduced, so buy with caution.

SHRINE CHAMPAGNE (ROCHESTER)

Shown is one of three known stemmed champagnes manufactured by the U.S. Glass Company, to be given away at Shrine Conventions (a rare toothpick is also known). The 1911 Rochester, New York Champagne has painted scenes of Rochester and Pittsburgh with gilt decoration. The other champagnes are the 1910 New Orleans and Tobacco Leaf (Louisville, Ky. — 1909). Each is a premium example of the glass maker's skill.

Seacoast Pintray

Seaweed

Six-S...

Seaweed Lamp

Shell

Shell and Jewel

Shrine Champagne (Rochester)

SMOOTH PANELS

While this Imperial design is very much like the Flute #3 pattern, there are small differences. The most obvious one is that the Flute panels are concave while the Smooth Panel ones are convex. Found in water sets in marigold, green and smoke, or an 11″ vase of pearl opalescent. This same vase has been seen in marigold, amber, smoke, green, and purple. The example shown has the Imperial "iron cross" mark.

SNOW FANCY

Known in small bowls as well as a creamer and sugar breakfast set, this scarce near-cut pattern is one not many collectors are familiar with. The bowl has been seen in green as well as a frosty white and the breakfast set is shown in marigold; other colors may exist but I haven't seen them. It is a McKee product.

SODA GOLD

Much confused with Tree of Life and Crackle shown elsewhere in this book, Imperial's Soda Gold differs from either in that the veins are much more pronounced and are highly raised from the stippled surface. It is found only on short candlesticks, a rare 9″ bowl, and beautiful water sets in marigold or smoke.

SOLDIERS AND SAILORS (ILL.)

One of two known such commemorative plates, this is the Illinois version. It features the Soldiers and Sailors Home in Quincy, Illinois, and measures 7½″. On the exterior is found Fenton's Berry and Leaf Circle design. The colors known are marigold, amethyst, and blue.

SOUTACHE PLATE

I've long believed this to be a Northwood pattern and while I've seen it on both bowls and lamp shades, this is the first footed plate I've run across. It measures 8¾″ in diameter and has peach opalescent edging. The foot is a dome base and is of clear glass.

SPIRAL CANDLE

Like the Premium Candlesticks also made by Imperial, these heavy, practical candlesticks were sold in pairs and were made in green, smoke, and marigold. They measure 8¼″ from the base to the top, and as far as I know, did not have a console bowl to match. The smoke coloring is particularly beautiful with many fiery highlights.

Smooth Panels

Snow Fancy

Soda Gold

Soldiers and Sailors (Ill.)

Soutache Plate

Spiral Candle

SPIRALEX

This is the name used in England to describe these lovely vases so I've continued using it. The colors are marigold, amethyst, green, and blue, and all I've seen are outstanding with very rich iridescence. Sizes range from 8″ to 14″.

SPLIT DIAMOND

I'm very happy to show the complete table set in this Davisons pattern, for while the creamer is easily found, the covered butter and sugar is quite scarce in this country. The only color is a good strong marigold with fine luster and superior mold.

SPRINGTIME

In many ways this pattern is similar to Northwood's Raspberry pattern, especially since both are bordered at the bottom with versions of a basketweave. Springtime, however, is really its own master and bears panels of wheat, flowers, and butterflies above and throughout the basketweave. Found in berry sets, table sets and very scarce water sets in marigold, green, amethyst, and also in pastels, Springtime is a very desirable pattern.

STAG AND HOLLY

This is probably the best known animal pattern in all of Carnival Glass other than the Peacock and certainly it remains one of Fenton's best efforts. Often brought out at Christmas time, the Stag and Holly is found mainly on footed bowls, rare footed plates, and rare rose bowls. Colors are marigold, blue, green, amethyst, aqua, peach opalescent, and red.

STAR AND FAN VASE

While I've been privileged to see the two Imperial marigold vases shown, I'm told a beautiful cobalt blue example also exists and let me add, it must be something, for the two marigold ones shown are very beautiful examples of the glass maker's art. The glass itself is thick and very clear. The lustre is rich and even and the design is flawless. Star and Fan is 9½″ tall.

STAR AND FILE

Very much like Star Medallion in concept, Imperial's Star and File doesn't have the Cann effect, but uses panels of file, hobstars, and sunbursts in a well balanced design. Found in bowls, breakfast sets, a water set, a wine decanter set, handled vases, a rare rosebowl, and a large compote, Star and File is known in marigold, smoke, purple and green.

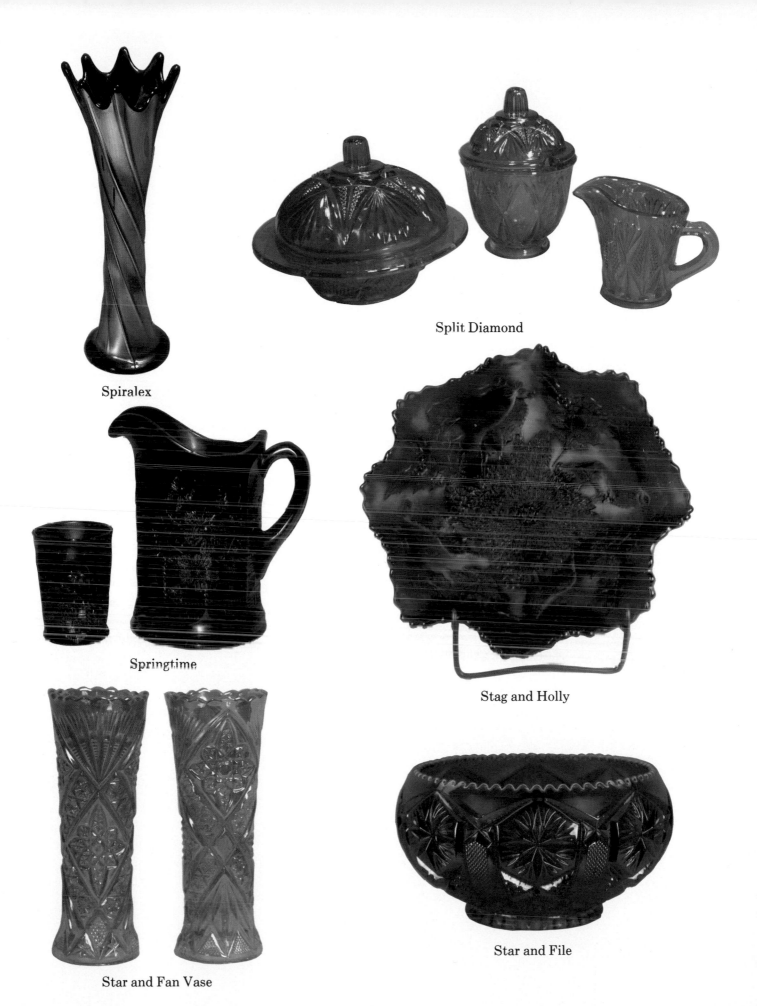

Spiralex

Split Diamond

Springtime

Stag and Holly

Star and Fan Vase

Star and File

STAR COASTER

While there may not be a great deal of inventiveness to this English pattern, it certainly serves a useful purpose and does it with a good deal of attractiveness. The clear center shows off the star on the base quite well and the two tiny rows of rope edging add a bit of interest. Marigold is the only color I've heard about.

STAR FISH

As you can see, this little compote is a real cutie. The design is strong and interesting and the quality is top notch. Star Fish is from the Dugan Company and is seen in marigold, green, purple, and the beautiful peach opalescent.

STAR MEDALLION

Star Medallion is a much overlooked, but well designed near cut Imperial pattern. Apparently it was a very popular pattern in its day for it is found in many shapes, including bowls of all shapes, a table set, a handled celery, a 9″ plate, milk pitcher, punch cup, tumbler, goblet, and a very beautiful compote. Colors are a rich marigold, smoke and occasionally a beautiful helios green.

STAR OF DAVID

For some unknown reason, only small amounts of this beautiful Imperial pattern must have been produced, for it is seldom seen today. As you can see, it is simply a Star of David half-stippled on a plain background with smooth ribbing to the edge of the bowl. The example shown measures 8¾″ in diameter and is the famous helios green of Imperial with a silver finish, but the pattern is also known in marigold, smoke and purple. The exterior carries the Arcs pattern.

STAR OF DAVID AND BOWS

The Northwood version of this figure (Imperial also produced a Star of David bowl) is a very attractive dome footed bowl and is a tribute to the Jewish religion. The Star is interlaced and is beaded while a graceful border of flowers, tendrils and bows edge the stippled center. The exterior is the Vintage pattern and the colors are marigold, green and amethyst.

STAR SPRAY

Now and then this Imperial pattern is found in crystal or marigold carnival glass; however, the smoke color is quite scarce and this is the only example I ever found of the complete bride's basket. The bowl measures 7½″ in diameter and has a beautiful finish. The metal holder is nicely done, having a fine gold overspray and tiny rosettes with leaves on the handles.

Star Coaster

Star Fish

Star Modallion

Star of David

Star of David and Bows

Star Spray

STARFLOWER

I certainly wish I could provide a manufacturer of this rare and beautiful pitcher (no tumblers known) but I can't. Known in both blue and marigold, the pitcher has turned up in two heights. The mold work is outstanding and the design flawless. Please notice how much the design resembles that of Millersburg's Little Star pattern.

STIPPLED DIAMOND SWAG

This beautifully designed English compote seems to be the only shape known in this pattern and while Mrs. Presznick reports green and blue ones, I've seen only the rich marigold shown. The compote is 5″ tall and measures 5¾″ across the top, with a 3½″ base.

STIPPLED RAMBLER ROSE NUT BOWL

While this pattern may have been made by someone else, I have a strong hunch this was an unmarked Northwood item. In size it resembles the Grape Delight nut bowl but has only three strange feet, unlike any others I've seen in Carnival Glass. They end in flattened knobs. The coloring is good and both the inside and outside are iridized. This scarce item is 4″ tall. It is found in a beautiful blue as well as the marigold shown.

STIPPLED RAYS

While Stippled Rays was used by both Northwood and Millersburg too, the Fenton version is perhaps the most commonly known and is available in bowls, bon-bons, compotes, plates, creamers and sugars. The colors found are marigold, amethyst, green, blue, and a rare red.

STIPPLED RAYS

As you can readily see, the Imperial version of Stippled Rays is quite different than that of the Fenton Company in that the edges are evenly scalloped and the pieces are footed. Known only in a breakfast set to date, I suspect other unreported shapes exist. The colors are marigold, smoke, and helios green.

STIPPLED RAYS (AND VARIANTS)

Every carnival-producing glass company had a stippled rays pattern and it is probably the most common motif in the entire field of iridized glass other than the grape. Northwood had several versions. The one shown is a variant. The most unusual aspects of the bowl are the reversed N and the exterior pattern which is a Greek Key and Scales. As you can see, it is a beautiful fiery amethyst and the bowl is dome footed. Stippled Rays was made in most colors and several shapes.

Starflower

Stippled Diamond Swag

Stippled Rambler Rose Nut Bowl

Stippled Rays

Stippled Rays

Stippled Rays and Variants

STIPPLED STRAWBERRY

While this pattern has been reported previously in a tumbler only, it obviously wasn't limited to that shape, and it is a real pleasure to show this rare spittoon shape. It stands 3½″ tall and measures 4½″ across its widest part. The coloring is nothing spectacular but adequate. Along the spittoon's lip is a checkerboard pattern. The manufacturer is the Jenkins Company.

STORK ABC PLATE

I'm certain many as collectors will question my placing this pattern as an Imperial one. But on close examination this pattern and that of the Bellaire Souvenir bowl are almost identical in makeup. It is my guess both patterns were turned out late in the Imperial line and each are rather scarce. The only color is marigold.

STORK AND RUSHES

Stork and Rushes is another pattern whose shards were found in the Dugan diggings and since it has features that are typical of Northwood, I'm afraid it's difficult to state whether Dugan or Northwood made this pattern. At any rate, it is available in berry sets, punch sets, water sets, hats and mugs. I've seen only marigold, purple, and blue with purple probably the hardest color to find.

STORK VASE

Much like the Swirl vase in concept, the Stork Vase was made by Imperial and is usually found in a pale marigold glass. The Stork is on one side only, with stippling covering the other side. The Stork Vase stands 7½″ tall.

STRAWBERRY

This cute little bon-bon shape has been seen in all sorts of glass including crystal, custard, milk glass, and carnival glass where the colors range from marigold, cobalt, amethyst, and green to the rare red amberina shown and a good rich all red. The design qualities aren't all that good, but the iridescence is usually adequate and on the whole, this Fenton bon-bon comes off nicely.

STRAWBERRY

Like its close relatives, Grape and Blackberry Wreaths this beautiful pattern is the culmination of the design. Its detailing is much finer than either of the other patterns and the glass is exceptional. The coloring is a true grape purple and the iridescence is a light even gold. Like other Millersburg patterns, the shapes vary but this deep tri-cornered bowl with candy-ribbon edge is my favorite. A rare compote exists in the usual colors.

Stippled Strawberry

Stork ABC Plate

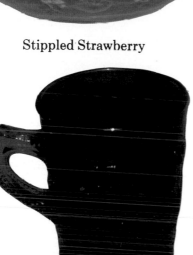

Stork and Rushco

Stork Vase

Strawberry

Strawberry

STRAWBERRY

Available in only bowls of various sizes and plates in either flat or hand grip styles, this well-known Northwood pattern comes either plain or stippled. On the stippled version, there are three narrow rings around the outer edge; these are absent on the plain pieces. Colors are both vivid and pastel with the purple showing off the pattern to its best.

STRAWBERRY EPERGNE

The Strawberry Epergne is very much like the Fish Net one also made by Dugan; however the former is much rarer and has not been reported in peach opalescent yet. As you can see the bowl exterior is plain and the base is domed.

STRAWBERRY SCROLL

Much like the rare Lily of the Valley in design, this rare Fenton water set is a real beauty that can stand along side of the best designs in Carnival Glass. The shape, like that of the Blueberry set, is very artistic also. Colors reported are marigold and blue but I suspect amethyst and green are possibilities.

STRAWBERRY INTAGLIO

I showed this pattern in my first glass book as a questionable Millersburg pattern. Since then we've been able to trace it to the Northwood Company through both a "goofus" bowl and a gilt decorated one, both bearing the famous trade-mark. The glass is thick, the design deeply impressed and the iridescence only so-so. I've seen large and small bowls only.

STREAM OF HEARTS

The same heart shape employed by Fenton on the Heart and Vine, and Heart and Trees designs is found here on the scale filler swirls that form a peacock's tail. Usually found on the compote shape, often with Persian Medallion as an exterior companion, Stream of Hearts is available on a 10″ footed bowl also. Colors are marigold, blue and white.

STRETCH

While we couldn't take the time to show all the shapes made in Fenton's vast stretch line, I wanted to show these matching breakfast set pieces because they so typify the Fenton style and because they are so scarce. Please note the contrasting colored handles are not iridized.

Strawberry

Strawberry Epergne

Strawberry Scroll

Strawberry Intaglio

Stream of Hearts

Stretch

STRUTTING PEACOCK

The only shapes in this Westmoreland pattern are the creamer and sugar and the only colors I've heard about are green or amethyst. The design is much like Shell and Jewel, also a Westmoreland product, but beware; these have been reproduced.

SUN-GOLD EPERGNE

Although I question the origin of this beautiful epergne, I don't for one minute doubt its desirability. The base is of highly polished pierced brass while the bowl and lily are of an unusual pinkish-marigold carnival glass. The epergne is 12″ tall and the bowl has a 9¼″ diameter. The glass is clear and mirror-like and has good even iridescence. This piece is probably Australian.

SUNFLOWER

Sunflower must have been a very popular pattern in its day, for numerous examples have survived to the present time. It's quite easy to see why it was in demand. It's a pretty, well designed Northwood pattern that holds iridescence beautifully. The bowl is footed and carries the very pleasing Meander pattern on the exterior. It is also found, rarely, on a plate. The colors are marigold, green, and amethyst.

SUNFLOWER AND DIAMOND

Long felt to be a Jenkins pattern this well done vase is now known to be of English origin and an example in blue with the Sowerby "peacock" mark has been reported. The usual color is a good marigold. The pattern is all intaglio and very deep.

SUNFLOWER PINTRAY

Like its companion piece the Seacoast Pintray, this Millersburg item joins the list of a select few. It is 5¼″ long and 4½″ wide and also rests on a collar base. The most unique feature is of course, the open handle and the colors are marigold, purple, amethyst, and a rich green.

SUNKEN HOLLYHOCK

Probably found more readily than the other "Gone With the Wind" lamps, Sunken Hollyhock can be found in marigold (often with a caramel coloring) and a very rare red. The lamp stands an impressive 25″ tall and certainly is a show stopper.

Strutting Peacock

Sun-Gold Epergne

Sunflower

Sunflower and Diamond

Sunflower Pintray

Sunken Hollyhock

SUNRAY COMPOTE

These small compotes, found on marigold over milk glass, are very pretty in their own plain way. Fenton made many such items and I strongly feel this compote came from that company also.

SUPERB DRAPE

The title of this beautiful piece of glass is certainly appropriate — it is superb! About 6½″ tall and 7″ in diameter, this very rare vase is a true aqua with a rich even butterscotch iridization. The gently rolling top shows a mellow opalescence as does the base. All in all, this Northwood creation is a rare beauty that would grace any collection superbly!

SWAN, PASTEL

Of all the shards of patterns I catalogued from the Dugan dump site, I'm sure this pattern surprised me more than any other. For years I considered these small novelties either Fenton or Westmoreland products with my vote leaning toward the latter. However, we now can say with some positiveness that they are Dugan. Found in pink, ice blue, ice green, marigold, peach, and purple, the darker colors and peach are the scarcest and demand greater prices.

SWEETHEART

Besides the rare and beautiful covered cookie jar shown, this Cambridge pattern is known in a very rare tumbler shape in marigold. The cookie jar has been seen in marigold, green, and amethyst and as you can see, the mold work and finish are superior.

SWIRL (IMPERIAL)

This 7″ vase is shown in old Imperial catalogs and I've heard of it in marigold, smoke, green, and white. The design is nothing outstanding, but the useful shape and the iridescence are adequate.

SWIRL

I've seen this pattern on a beautiful tankard water set and the mug shape in marigold. The tumbler is shown in the Owens book in green and is known in amethyst. While the tumblers are often marked, the mug isn't. Now and then the tankard pitcher is found with enameled flowers added. Naturally the pitcher is scarce and the mug is considered rare.

Sunray Compote

Superb Drape

Swan Pastel

Sweetheart

Swirl (Imperial)

Swirl

SWIRLED FLUTE VASE

This cute little Fenton vase is a real charmer for such a simplistic design. The wide panel is quite pronounced at the base and the color and iridescence are quite good. These little vases average about 9″ in height and are found in red, marigold, green, amethyst, blue, and white.

SWIRL CANDLESTICK

This very attractive candlestick is the same pattern as the rare mug I showed in previous books and was apparently a product of either Northwood or Dugan. While other colors may exist, I haven't heard of any. The luster is top notch and the glass, quality all the way.

SWIRL HOBNAIL

This is a little Millersburg jewel in either the rosebowl or the ladies spittoon and once you own either piece, wild horses couldn't drag it away. The glass is simply sparkling and the iridescence outstanding. The spittoon has an irregular scalloped edge opening and both shapes have a many rayed base. The usual colors prevail, but the green is extremely difficult to locate. Swirl Hobnail can also be found in a vase shape.

TAFFETA LUSTRE CANDLESTICKS

These very rare Fostoria candlesticks were manufactured in 1916 or 1917 (according to an old Fostoria catalog) in colors of amber, blue, green, crystal or orchid. They were part of a "flower set" which included a center piece bowl 11″ in diameter. The candlesticks themselves came in 2, 4, 6, 9 and 12 sizes and as you can see, these still have the original paper labels on the bottom. When held to the light, the ultra-violet color is fantastic and the iridescence is heavy and rich. Fostoria made very small amounts of iridized glass and certainly these examples of their Taffeta Lustre line are quite rare.

TEN MUMS

Found on beautiful water sets, large impressive bowls, and rare plates, Fenton's Ten Mums is a very realistic pattern. The mold work is unusually fine, especially on the bowl shape. Colors are marigold, cobalt blue, green, peach opalescent, and white but not all shapes are found in all colors.

THIN RIB AND DRAPE

Much like the other Thin Rib vases, this one has an interior drape pattern, adding to the interest. It can be found in several colors including marigold, green, and amethyst. I suspect Fenton is the maker, but can't be sure.

Swirled Flute Vase

Swirl Candlestick

Swirl Hobnail

Taffeta Lustre Candlesticks

Ten Mums

Thin Rib and Drape

THISTLE

Fairly typical of many Fenton bowl patterns, Thistle is artistically true with the thistles and leaves realistic and graceful. Found on bowls, plates and a rare compote, the colors seen are marigold, green, blue and occasionally amethyst. Now and then a bowl appears with advertising on the base.

THISTLE AND THORN

British in origin, this nicely designed pattern is found on a variety of shapes, all footed, including bowls, sugars, creamers, plates, and nut bowls. Colors are usually marigold but I've had blue reported.

THISTLE BANANA BOAT

This beautiful Fenton banana boat is another of the underrated patterns in Carnival Glass. Massive in concept, bold in design with the thistle on the interior and cattail and waterlily outside, the four-footed Banana Boat is usually found on marigold, green, or cobalt blue. The iridescence is quite heavy, usually with much gold.

THISTLE VASE

What a pretty little vase this is. Standing 6″ tall with a soft amber shading to the glass, the Thistle vase is a well-designed bit of color for vase lovers. The maker is unknown but is definitely English.

THREE FRUITS

So very close in design to the Northwood Fruits and Flowers pattern shown earlier in this book, the two substantial differences are the absence of the small flowers and the addition of an extra cluster of cherries to this pattern. Found in bowls of all sizes, including flat and footed ones, and average size plates. Northwood's Three Fruits is available in all vivid colors as well as pastels.

THREE FRUITS VARIANT

If you'll compare this beautiful 9″ plate with the Northwood version you'll see a good deal of similarities and some obvious differences. While this version has been credited to Fenton, I strongly suspect it was a Dugan product.

THREE-IN-ONE

Originally called "Number One" in the crystal line, this well-known Imperial bowl pattern (plates also exist) is always easy to spot because of the two rows of near cut diamond designs, separated by a center area of flutes. I've seen bowls in 4½″, 7½″, 8¾″ sizes, in colors of deep marigold, green, purple, and smoke. The iridescence is usually quite good and the glass heavy, clear and sparkling.

Thistle

Thistle and Thorn

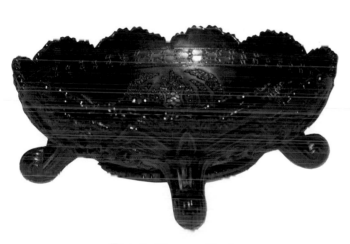

Thistle Banana Boat

Thistle Vase

Three Fruits

Three Fruits Variant

Three-In-One

THREE MONKEYS BOTTLE

I'm not sure how many of these are around but not many I'd guess. The one shown is the reported example in all the previous pattern books, so it may have only few brothers. The Three Monkeys bottle is of clear glass with **good** iridescence, stands 8″ tall and bears the words: "PATENT PENDING — 8 OZ." on the base. A rare find for bottle lovers.

THREE ROW VASE

I was very impressed when I saw this beautiful Imperial rarity. The color was truly fabulous and the iridescence fine enough to rival the Farmyard bowl. I have heard of only this one piece in beautiful purple, but others may exist. It is 8″ tall and 4½″ wide and the mold work is quite deep and sharp. There is also a variant called **Two Row** vase which is quite similar.

THUMBPRINT AND OVAL

Standing only 5½″ tall, this well-molded Imperial pattern is known in marigold and purple. Either color is scarce and Thumbprint and Oval is much sought.

THUNDERBIRD (SHRIKE)

Called Thunderbird in America, the bird shown is actually a Shrike. The flora is of course, wattle. This Australian pattern can be found in both large and small bowls in marigold or purple.

TIGER LILY

It really is a shame this well-done Imperial pattern was used only on the water set. It would have been quite effective on any number of other shapes, including table sets and punch sets. The mold work is some of Imperial's best, all intaglio, and very sharp and precise. Tiger Lily is found in marigold, green, and, rarely, purple. It has been reproduced in pastels, so beware!

TINY COVERED HEN

The Imperial novelty item shown is a really well-conceived miniature that until recently had not been reproduced; however, I saw one of these in a gift shop in blue glass (not carnival) not long ago. At any rate the one shown is old and rare. The coloring is a very nice clambroth, richly iridized with a fiery finish. It measures 3½″ long and 3¼″ tall.

TOMAHAWK

This lovely miniature (7¼″ long and 2″ wide) is a real "show stopper". Now known to have been a product of the Cambridge Glass Company, the rare Tomahawk is a very deep cobalt blue with heavy iridescence. It has been seen in pieces other than carnival glass and has been reproduced in aqua and vaseline glass, but as far as I know, no iridized reproductions were made.

Three Monkeys Bottle

Three Row Vase

Thumbprint and Oval

Tiger Lily

Thunderbird (Shrike)

Tiny Covered Hen

Tomahawk

TORNADO

Perhaps because it is one of the most unusual vases in all of carnival glass, Northwood's Tornado is always a favorite with collectors. Available in both plain and ribbed, the size may vary considerably and I've seen a mini-version in marigold. The colors are marigold, green, purple, white, and ice blue. The Northwood trade-mark is found on the inside of the vase.

TORNADO VARIANT

This extremely rare variant is one inch taller than the regular Tornado vase. The base closely resembles that of Northwood's Corn Vase and the top is tightly crimped. The only color reported is a deep rich marigold, iridized both inside and out.

TOWN PUMP

Certainly there isn't one collector of carnival glass who isn't familiar with this very famous pattern. The Town Pump is almost 7″ tall and is mostly on purple, although marigold and green are found in limited quantities. The design is simple but very pleasing — ivy twining over a stippled background with a crude tree bark spout and handle. No carnival glass collection would be complete without this pattern and certainly it deserves a prominent place in any Northwood collection.

TRACERY

This pattern comes as quite a surprise to many Millersburg fans because of its delicate patterning, but Millersburg it certainly is. It is found on bon-bons of rather deep, oval shape and is usually seen in green or amethyst. It measures 7½″ long and 5½″ wide. The base is 3″ in diameter and has a many rayed center. The exterior is plain and has two mold marks.

TREE BARK

As you can see, this is a simplistic pattern, turned out as a giveaway item or an inexpensive one. The only shapes I've heard of are water sets with either open or lidded pitchers and the only color is marigold, usually of a deep, rich hue. While it certainly does not show the artistry the Imperial Company was known for, Tree Bark does fulfill its purpose of being an available bit of color for the average housewife's table.

TREE OF LIFE

There has always been a great deal of confusion surrounding this pattern, and Crackle and Soda Gold patterns, because they are so similar, but there is really no need for the confusion. As you can see, Tree of Life has no stippling whatsoever, thus the filler area is plain. The pitcher shown is a scarce shape in this pattern, and as you can see, the iridescence is thin and light. The shapes known are water sets, plates and perfume bottles.

TREE TRUNK

Simple but effective is the bark-like pattern for this popular Northwood vase. Apparently it was a well-liked pattern when it was being manufactured for many examples exist in sizes from 8″ to tall 20″ ones. The colors are marigold, blue, purple, green and white.

Tornado

Tornado Variant

Town Pump

Tracery

Tree Bark

Tree of Life

Tree Trunk

TRIADS (and Towers vase)

Triads is a product of Sowerbys and is found in a covered butter dish, creamer, sugar, celery, and spooner (both shown). The only color reported is a good rich marigold. The other small hat shape shown is called Towers and is a vase pattern also from Sowerbys.

TROPICANA VASE

The maker of this intriguing vase is unknown, but I suspect it may be English. It stands 9″ tall and has a very rich marigold coloring.

TROUT AND FLY

Of course, this is a companion piece to the Big Fish pattern and except for the added fly and a few changes in the water lilies and blossoms, is much the same. These bowls usually measure about 9¼″ in diameter and have a wide panel exterior. The detail is good and the coloring excellent. The shape may vary and even square bowls and a rare plate shape have been found in this Millersburg pattern.

TULIP SCROLL

I've seen only two of these vases, one in green, 11½″ tall and one in a very rich amethyst, 7″ tall. Recent evidence indicates this to be a Millersburg pattern and the endings of the design exactly like the base design of Zig Zag and Millersburg Vintage bowls.

TWINS

Like Imperial's Fashion pattern, Twins is another geometric design manufactured in large quantities in berry sets, a rare bride's basket, and the familiar fruit bowl and stand. Pieces have been found in a good rich marigold and a very beautiful smoke and the berry set has been found in green, as shown. Needless to say, a purple fruit bowl and stand would be a treasure!

TWO FLOWERS

Once again the scale filler, water lilies, and blossoms are used by Fenton to form an artistic presentation. Known in footed and flat bowls of various sizes and a scarce rose bowl shape, Two Flowers is seen in blue, marigold, amethyst, green, and occasionally white.

TWO FRUITS

Once this Fenton pattern was felt to be an Imperial product but we know from old advertisements that it came from Fenton. The background is Fenton's Stippled Rays and, as you can see, there are four sections to the divided bon-bon. Each section contains one fruit — either a pear or an apple. Colors I've heard about are marigold, blue, and amethyst but certainly green may exist.

Tropicana Vase

Trout and Fly

Triads (and Towers Vase)

Tulip Scroll

Twins

Two Flowers

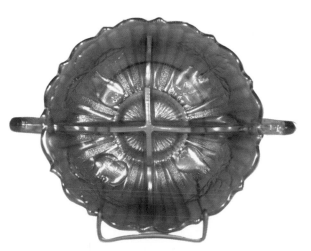

Two Fruits

209

TWO FRUITS

Here is a Northwood pattern so unique and so very rare, it is not listed in the two major pattern guides. Shown is the spooner in a rich cobalt blue. It last sold in the 1977 Wishard auction. I know of one other piece in this pattern, a lidless sugar. Shown is the cherry side; the other pattern on the opposite side shows two peaches. The spooner measures 6¼″ x 4½″ and bears the Northwood trademark.

URN VASE

This unusually shaped vase has been seen in white as well as marigold carnival glass and is a product of the Imperial Company. It stands 9″ tall and has a finely grained stippling over the surface.

VENETIAN

While credited to the Cambridge company, there is evidence that this pattern was iridized at the Millersburg factory. It is shown in old Cambridge ads, however, and was often used as a lamp base. Colors are green and a scarce marigold. The base design is quite similar to the Hobstar and Feather rosebowl.

VICTORIAN

Let me say in the beginning I think this is one of the most under-rated patterns in the entire field of carnival glass. In size it is generous and commanding, being some 11″ in diameter. Also, the glass is heavy, the color is deep and rich, and iridescence often rivals that of the Farmyard bowl. Indeed, I can not understand why it doesn't bring raves since it is relatively scarce and always adds a great deal of class to any collection. Purple is the only color I've ever seen in this Northwood pattern.

VINEYARD

Here is another pattern whose shards I catalogued from the Dugan diggings, but actually it didn't come as too much of a surprise. The same design was made in 1905 in crystal, opaque glass, and opalescent wear under the name, Grape and Leaf.* Known in iridescent glass, in a water set only, the colors are marigold, purple and rarely peach opalescent. Often the tumblers are poorly formed and the glass tends toward being bubbled.

VINING LEAF

There are two variants of this English pattern — one with small berries along portions of the stylized leaves. The examples shown, a rather small bud vase and an ample lady's spittoon, give us the pattern nicely. Please note the frosted effect around the leaves.

VINTAGE BANDED

Often seen in the mug shape, this Dugan pattern is rather scarce in the footed pitcher shape and the tumbler is rare and much sought. Please note the grapes are almost identical to those found on the Golden Grape pattern and the banding is quite similar to that found on the Dugan pattern called Apple Blossoms.

Two Fruits

Urn Vase

Venetian

Victorian

Vineyard

Vining Leaf

Vintage Banded

VINTAGE

Vintage was the Fenton Company's primary grape pattern and as such can be found in a wide range of shapes, including bowls, plates, rose bowls, compotes, punch sets, ferneries, and a one-lily epergne. Shown is the Vintage fernery in a rare red. Other colors known are marigold, blue, green, amethyst, amber, pastel marigold, and amberina.

VINTAGE

What makes Vintage unique is the hobnail exterior (the hobnail and the honey-comb seem to have been patterns used as standard fillers by Millersburg). It has a many-rayed star in the base and is usually seen on medium size, shallow bowls. The Millersburg Vintage pattern is a scarce one and is certainly a credit to any collection. Colors are green, marigold, amethyst, and blue; and both 9″ and 5″ bowls are known.

VIOLET BASKETS

Here are two of the dainty little baskets designed to hold small bouquets like violets. One has its own glass handle, while the other fits into a handled sleeve. The File pattern in the glass is much like that on some Stork and Rushes pieces and I suspect both of these baskets come from the Dugan Company.

VOTIVE LIGHT

Also bearing the strange M-inside-a-C mark like Oklahoma, this very hard to find novelty has a beautiful marigold finish. It stands 4¼″ tall and is a Holy Water vase. The side shown is the Bleeding Heart of Jesus. On the opposite side is a raised cross measuring nearly 2″ tall. Again I list Imperial as the speculative maker.

WAFFLE BLOCK

This Imperial pattern was originally made in many shapes. The pitcher is hard to come by and of course the tumblers are rather rare, but other shapes, including a handled basket, rose bowl, punch set, vases, bowls, parfait glass, and shakers are known.

WATER LILY

Found on bon-bons and flat and footed berry sets, Water Lily is similar to Lotus and Grape, Pond Lily and Thistle and Lotus. They each give a feeling of a small lily pond. The usual lotus-like flowers are present along with water-lily blossoms, leaves, and small vine-like flora. Colors known are marigold, blue, green, amethyst, amber, white, and red.

WATER LILY AND CATTAILS

While both Fenton and Northwood had versions of this pattern, the Fenton one is best known and is available in more shapes, including water sets, table sets, berry sets, and a rare spittoon whimsey. Colors are marigold and amethyst, but certainly blue or green may exist but have not been reported.

Vintage

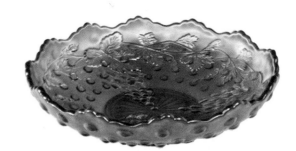

Vintage

Violet
Baskets

Voltive Light

Waffle Block

Water Lily

Water Lily and Cattails

WATERLILY AND CATTAILS

Here is a pattern used in different degrees by both the Northwood and Fenton Companies and at times it's rather hard to tell who made what. The obvious Fenton rendition is the exterior pattern used on the Thistle banana boat, but it is believed they made other shapes in Water Lily and Cattails, including a whimsey toothpick. This is the Northwood water set.

WATER LILY AND DRAGONFLY

This large (10½″) shallow bowl and matching frog is called a flower set and was used much like an epergne. A large flannel flower is under the frog. In Australia these are also called "float bowls."

WHEAT

Make no mistake about it, this is a very rare Northwood pattern, known in only a covered sweetmeat (2 known) and a single bowl in colors of green and amethyst. Surfacing in carnival glass circles only in the last couple of years, these rarities have caused much excitement and brought astonishing prices where they've been shown. The sweetmeat is the same shape as the Northwood Grape pattern. What a pity we don't have more of this truly important pattern.

WHIRLING LEAVES

What a simple but effective pattern for large bowls! Four flowing leaves and four star-like blossoms — what could be simpler. Please note that the flowers are very much like those found on the Little Stars bowls. This pleasing pattern is not especially difficult to find and does not sell for nearly as much as most Millersburg patterns but it is worth owning.

WHIRLING STAR

Very little is ever said of this Imperial near cut pattern and perhaps it is just too much of a good thing, for there are sections of hobstars, fine cut buttons, file, diamond file, and whirling star shapes. Found mostly on large bowls and compotes the only colors I've seen are marigold and smoke.

WHITE OAK

After years of doubt about the maker of this rare tumbler (no pitcher known), I'm half convinced it was a Dugan product. The bark-like background and the general shape are much like the Vineyard tumbler. Of course I could be wrong.

WIDE PANEL

Like the other major carnival glass companies, Imperial produced a Wide Panel pattern. These are found primarily in goblets of two sizes and a covered candy jar. Colors known are marigold, ice blue, ice green, vaseline white, pink, and red. Most have a stretch effect around the edge.

Waterlily and Cattails

Water Lily and Dragonfly

Wheat

Whirling Leaves

Whirling Star

White Oak

Wide Panel

WIDE PANEL EPERGNE

This beauty is the most stately epergne in Carnival glass and is a product of the Northwood factory. Colors are white, marigold, green, amethyst, and the ultra-rare aqua opalescent one shown.

WIDE RIB VASE

While several glass companies produced these wide rib vases, the one shown came from the Dugan factory. Colors I've seen are marigold, green, blue, amethyst, smoke, white, amber, peach opalescent, and aqua opalescent.

WILD BLACKBERRY

Very much in design like the other Fenton Blackberry patterns, this is strictly a bowl pattern easily identified by the four center leaves and the wheat-like fronds around the outer edges. Colors are marigold, blue, green, and amethyst. The exterior has the wide panel pattern.

WILD FLOWER

This deeply cupped, clover-based compote is just over 6″ tall and is 4½″ wide. The very graceful pattern of four large leaves, four small leaves, and eight blossoms is quite effective. The iridescence is found only on the inside of the compote and has the usual radium finish. This is not an easy compote to find and anyone having one should be most proud. This Millersburg pattern is found in marigold, green, amethyst, and the rare vaseline shown.

WILD LOGANBERRY PITCHER (DEWBERRY)

Here's a sight to excite any pitcher lover's interest, for I've never heard of another of these! The finish is a good, strong marigold over milk glass, highly iridized inside and out. The Wild Loganberry pitcher has three mold lines and stands 8″ tall. The design is repeated on each side and in the back. It is my belief that this was part of a cider set made by the Fenton Company and had cider goblets rather than glasses.

WILD ROSE

This well-known Northwood pattern is used on the exterior of two types of bowls. The first is an average flat bowl, often with no interior pattern. The second, however, is an unusual footed bowl, rather small, with an edge of open work in fan-like figures. Certainly, the intricacy of this open work took much care and skill. The colors are marigold, amethyst, green, and occasionally pastels.

WILD ROSE LAMP

This very scarce lamp is found in three sizes and three colors, amethyst, green and marigold. The font is of clear glass but the remainder of the lamp is well-iridized. The Wild Rose pattern is well raised and meandering around the base of the lamp is a pattern of sunken dots. Occasionally one of these lamps is found with three medallions on the underside. These medallions contain portraits of three ladies believed to be wives of the three major stockholders of the Millersburg Company. One of these lamps would be a credit to any glass collection and certainly deserves top billing in a collection of Millersburg glass.

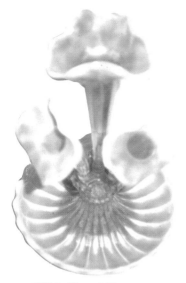

Wide Panel Epergne

Wide Rib Vase

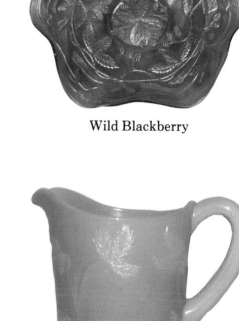

Wild Blackberry

Wild Flower

Wild Loganberry Pitcher

Wild Rose

Wild Rose Lamp

WILD ROSE SYRUP

Seen only in marigold of rich color and adequate lustering, the Wild Rose Syrup is very attractive. The maker is thus far unknown, but the mold work is quite similar to that of many of Harry Northwood's products. Measuring 6½" tall, the Syrup holds 12 fluid ounces and has a metal top.

WILD STRAWBERRY

One might think of this as the "grown-up" version of the regular Northwood Strawberry since it is much the same. The primary difference is the addition of the blossoms to the patterning and, of course, the size of the bowl itself; which is about 1½" larger in diameter. I have seen two exterior designs used. The most common by far is the standard basketweave, while rarely we encounter the Jeweled Heart pattern. This latter pattern really adds a good deal of class to the whole. The colors are rich, vivid greens and purples.

WINDFLOWER

Not one but two shards of this pattern were excavated at the Dugan site, including a marigold bit and a sizeable chunk of an ice blue nappy with a portion of the handle attached. To the best of my knowledge, this pattern has not been reported previously in pastels. Windflower is an uncomplicated, well balanced design with the background stippled and a geometric bordering device. The exterior is plain. Windflower is found on bowls, plates, and handled nappies. The colors are marigold, cobalt, and ice blue.

WINDMILL

Again, here is one of the best selling Imperial patterns, reproduced in the 60s. It is still rather popular with collectors of old carnival glass, especially in the darker colors. Originally, Windmill was made in a wide range of shapes, including berry sets, water sets, fruit bowls, pickle dishes, dresser trays, and the milk pitcher shown. The colors were marigold, green, purple, clambroth, and smoke.

WINDSOR FLOWER ARRANGER

Although the Windsor Flower Arranger is listed in old Imperial catalogs in crystal as #28411, apparently very few of these were ever iridized. The example shown is a beautiful clambroth color with sparkling iridescence. It measures 4¾" tall, with a lip diameter of 6" and is the only reported example I've seen. Of course, it must be classified as a rare item and will, I'm sure, cause a good deal of interest wherever it is shown.

WINE AND ROSES

Please note the similarities between this scarce Fenton cider set, the well-known Lotus and Grape pattern shown elsewhere in this book, and the very rare water set called Frolicking Bears (maker unknown). Wine and Roses can be found in marigold in both pitcher and wine and the wine is known in blue and the extremely rare aqua shown.

WISHBONE

I personally feel that this Northwood pattern is one of the most graceful in carnival glass. The lines just flow, covering much of the allowed space. Found on very scarce water sets, flat and footed bowls, plates, and a very stately one-lily epergne, Wishbone is usually accompanied by the basketweave pattern on the exterior. My favorite color is the ice blue, but Wishbone is available in marigold, green, purple, blue, white, and ice green. There is also a variant to this pattern.

Wild Rose Syrup

Wild Strawberry

Windflower

Windmill

Windsor Flower Arranger

Wine and Roses

Wishbone

WISHBONE AND SPADES

I've always had misgivings about attributing this pattern and I'm listing it here as a questionable Dugan one. As you can see, the design is a good one, well balanced and artistically sound. The shapes are berry sets and large and small plates and colors include peach opalescent, purple, and green.

WISTERIA

What a beautiful pattern this is! Certainly a first cousin to the Grape Arbor pattern in iridescent glass as well as the Lattice and Cherry pattern in crystal, Wisteria is unfortunately found only on water sets. While only tumblers in ice green have surfaced, both pitchers and tumblers are known in white and a really outstanding ice blue. What a shame no vivid colors are available in this Northwood masterpiece.

WOODEN SHOE

It seems as if good things come in bunches and that's how it's been with miniatures in this book. However, one could never tire of seeing them and they are rare so here is another. The Wooden Shoe is 4½" long and 3" high. Its coloring is a light watery amber and the glass is heavy.

WOODLANDS VASE

Once again I show a rare vase that is very impressive even though it measures only 5½" tall. The coloring is a rich marigold with heavy lustre and the pattern is all smooth and raised. The design has a simple, well-balanced attractiveness that raises it above the everyday. And, of course, not many are known.

WOODPECKER VASE

The Woodpecker vase is 8¼" long and measures 1⅝" across the top. The only color I've run into is marigold, usually of good color. Perhaps this is strictly a Dugan pattern, and if so, it would explain the lack of other colors or shapes. These vases were usually hung in doorways or used as auto vases and were quite popular in their day.

WREATHED CHERRY

For many years, collectors have been puzzled by certain pieces of this pattern turning up with the Diamond Glass Company trademark, notably the covered butter. Now, since the Dugan shards have been catalogued, it becomes apparent this was a Dugan pattern. Known in berry sets consisting of oval bowls, table sets, water sets, and a scarce toothpick holder, the colors are marigold, fiery amethyst, purple, and white (often with gilt). The toothpick has been widely reproduced in cobalt, white and marigold, so beware! The only color in the old ones is amethyst.

WREATH OF ROSES

Known in bon-bons with or without stems, compotes, bowls, and the punch set shown, Fenton's Wreath of Roses is a beautifully executed pattern. Two interior patterns are known. Colors are marigold, green, blue, amethyst, peach opalescent, and white. The luster is very fine and the mold work excellent.

Wishbone and Spades

Wisteria

Wooden Shoe

Woodlands Vase

Woodpecker Vase

Wreathed Cherry

Wreath of Roses

WREATH OF ROSES ROSEBOWL

I've never understood why this little rosebowl has been grouped with the Fenton Wreath of Roses as one and the same pattern when it is obviously so different. So when a large hunk of Wreath of Roses Rosebowl was found among the Dugan shards, the explanation became obvious. They simply are not the same pattern! Found in marigold and amethyst, the Wreath of Roses Rosebowl has superior mold work and adequate finish.

ZIG-ZAG

I suspect the same mold shape was used for this nicely done Fenton water set and the Fluffy Peacock pattern. The Zig Zag was brought along in the enameled Carnival period and can be found in marigold, blue, green, amethyst, ice green,and white. The floral work may vary slightly from piece to piece.

ZIG ZAG

This lovely Millersburg bowl pattern is an improved version of a stippled ray theme but with a twist, resulting in a beautiful sun burst effect. This, coupled with a curious star and fan design on the exterior base, creates a unique and intriguing pattern. On the amethyst bowl shown, the stippled zig-zag rays show much gold while the plain ones remain purplish. This gives an unbelievable richness to the design and raises it above the ordinary. Other colors are green and marigold.

ZIPPERED HEART

Recent evidence that this is an Imperial pattern is a catalog from the company illustrating the Zippered Heart pattern in crystal in many shapes, including table sets, vases, compotes, rosebowls, a milk pitcher, punch sets, and water sets. However, in iridized glass the shapes I've seen are a berry set and the famous Queen's vase. While a beautiful purple is most encountered, marigold is known.

ZIPPER LOOP

While the Zipper Loop lamp is the most frequently encountered or all the kerosene lamps, it is a scarce item in itself. Known in four sizes, including a small hand lamp, the Zipper Loop is found in a good rich marigold color as well as a sparkling smoke finish. It has been reproduced in the former in the large size, so be cautious when buying.

ZIPPER STITCH

The 9½" tray shown is part of a cordial set whose origin we **suspect** to be English. The pattern is quite distinct, all exterior and the coloring is very rich marigold. Besides the tray, there is a decanter with stopper, 10" tall and six cordials on stems, 3⅝" tall.

ZIPPER VARIANT

I suspect this nicely done covered sugar is of British origin, but can't be sure. The color is quite good as is the mold work. Note the interesting finial on the lid.

Wreath
of Roses
Rosebowl

Zig-Zag

Zig-Zag

Zippered Heart

Zipper Stitch

Zipper Variant

Zipper Loop

ᴜᴍ